CAMBRIDGE LIBRARY COLLECTION

Books of enduring scholarly value

History

The books reissued in this series include accounts of historical events and movements by eye-witnesses and contemporaries, as well as landmark studies that assembled significant source materials or developed new historiographical methods. The series includes work in social, political and military history on a wide range of periods and regions, giving modern scholars ready access to influential publications of the past.

Tibet, Tartary and Mongolia

Henry T. Prinsep (1792–1878) was the son of a prominent East India Company servant, and like his father, he spent much of his life in the East. He left Britain for Calcutta in 1809, at the age of seventeen, and stayed in India, working in a variety of roles, until his retirement in 1843. He wrote a number of books about India: in this work, published in 1851, he turns to the north of the subcontinent. Prinsep draws from travel narratives of the few explorers who had been to this territory – which corresponds to today's western China and Mongolia – to illustrate the lives of the people there. Using sources ranging from the thirteenth-century account by Marco Polo to eighteenth-century reports by French missionaries, Prinsep brings information on what was then a little-known world to a wider audience.

Cambridge University Press has long been a pioneer in the reissuing of out-of-print titles from its own backlist, producing digital reprints of books that are still sought after by scholars and students but could not be reprinted economically using traditional technology. The Cambridge Library Collection extends this activity to a wider range of books which are still of importance to researchers and professionals, either for the source material they contain, or as landmarks in the history of their academic discipline.

Drawing from the world-renowned collections in the Cambridge University Library, and guided by the advice of experts in each subject area, Cambridge University Press is using state-of-the-art scanning machines in its own Printing House to capture the content of each book selected for inclusion. The files are processed to give a consistently clear, crisp image, and the books finished to the high quality standard for which the Press is recognised around the world. The latest print-on-demand technology ensures that the books will remain available indefinitely, and that orders for single or multiple copies can quickly be supplied.

The Cambridge Library Collection will bring back to life books of enduring scholarly value (including out-of-copyright works originally issued by other publishers) across a wide range of disciplines in the humanities and social sciences and in science and technology.

Tibet, Tartary and Mongolia

Their Social and Political Condition,
and the Religion of Boodh, as There Existing

HENRY THOBY PRINSEP

 CAMBRIDGE
UNIVERSITY PRESS

CAMBRIDGE UNIVERSITY PRESS

Cambridge, New York, Melbourne, Madrid, Cape Town,
Singapore, São Paolo, Delhi, Tokyo, Mexico City

Published in the United States of America by Cambridge University Press, New York

www.cambridge.org
Information on this title: www.cambridge.org/9781108028738

This edition first published 1851
This digitally printed version 2011

ISBN 978-1-108-02873-8 Paperback

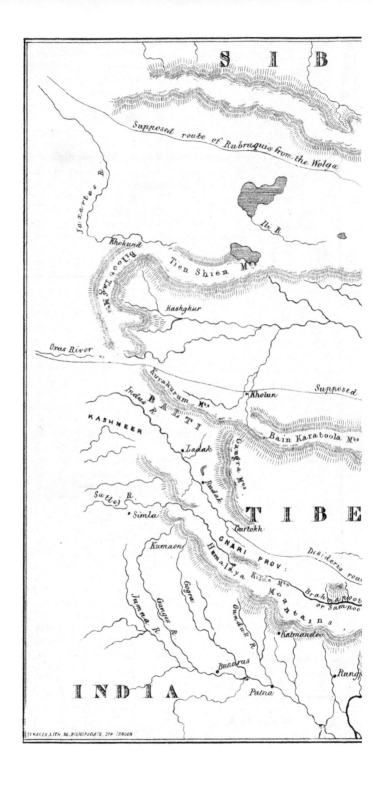

S I B

Supposed route of Rubraquis from the Wolga

Joxartes R.

Ili R.

Khokund

Tien Shien M^ts

Terrooll

Tag M^ts

Kashghur

Orus River

Kurakurum M^ts

Indus R.

Kholan

Supposed

KASHMEER

BALTI

Bain Karatoola M^ts

Ladak

Gangra M^ts

Rudak

Suttej R.

T I B E

Simla

Gartokh

Kumaon

GNARI PROV.

Desideris rou

Himalaya Kilas M^ts

Gogra

Montains

Brahmanpoot or Sampoo

Ganges R.

Jumna R.

Gunduk R.

Katmandoo

Bindrus

Rang

INDIA

Patna

STANER, LITH, 80, BISHOPSGATE, ST. LONDON.

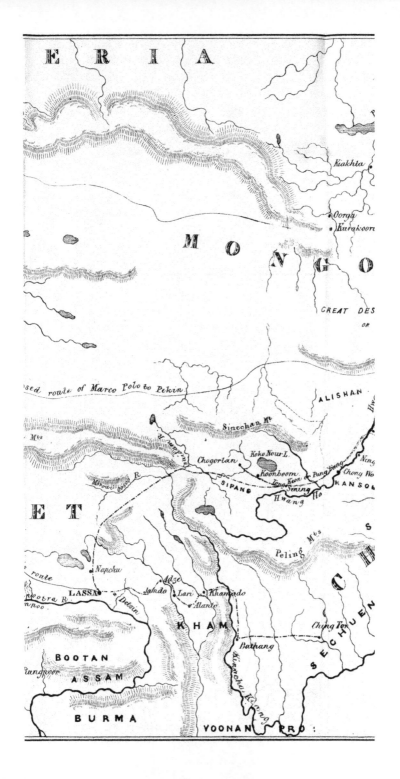

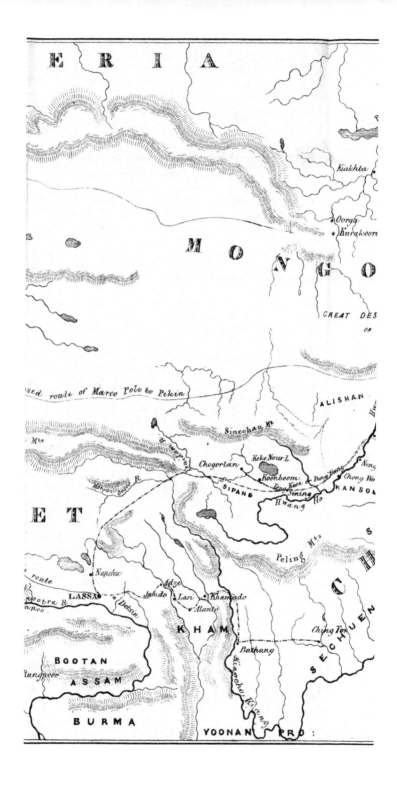

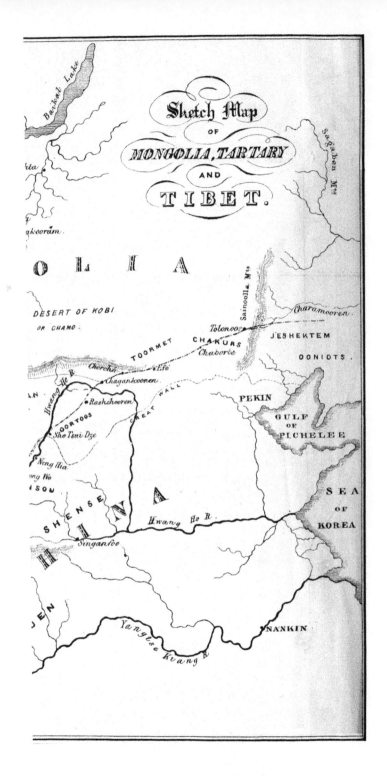

Sketch Map

OF

MONGOLIA, TARTARY

AND

TIBET.

Baikal Lake

Sagaben Mts

ta

akoorüm

OLIA

DESERT OF KOBI
OR CHAMO.

Saïnoolla Mts

Charamooren

Toloncor

JESHEKTEM

TOORMET

CHAKURS

Chaborée

OONIOTS.

Chercha

'sEfe

Chaganicoonen

Hwang Ho R

Rashchooren

PEKIN

ORTOOS

GREAT WALL

GULF
OF
PICHELEE

Sho Tsui Dze

Ning Hia

ong Ho

SOU

SHENSE

H N A

Hwang Ho R.

SEA

OF

KOREA

H

Singanfoo

EN

Yangtse Kiang R

NANKIN

TIBET, TARTARY AND MONGOLIA;

THEIR

SOCIAL AND POLITICAL CONDITION,

AND

THE RELIGION OF BOODH,

AS THERE EXISTING.

COMPILED FROM THE REPORTS OF ANCIENT AND MODERN TRAVELLERS, ESPECIALLY
FROM M. HUC'S REMINISCENCES OF THE RECENT JOURNEY OF HIMSELF
AND M. GABET, LAZARISTE MISSIONARIES OF MONGOLIA.

BY

HENRY T. PRINSEP, Esq.

LONDON:

WM. H. ALLEN & CO.,

7, LEADENHALL STREET.

1851.

TIBET, TARTARY AND MONGOLIA.

TIBET, Tartary, and Mongolia were unknown to
the ancients, except as lands of fable, occupied by
wandering Scythians. Tibet was the country
whence came the Indians of the Persian court,
who ate their dead, as told by Herodotus, and as
they themselves report to have been their ancient
custom. There is, however, no record of authentic travel into any region of the East, lying above
the Himalaya, and beyond the mountains in
which the Oxus and Jaxartes have their sources,
anterior to the journey of Father William Rubruquis to Karakurum, in the reign of Louis IX. of
France, and of Mangoo Khan, the grandson of
Jungeez Khan, of Tartary. This journey was un-
dertaken in A.D. 1253, at the time when King
Louis was in Syria engaged in a holy war. It had
its origin in an overture made, through a real or

B

pretended ambassador of the Khan of the Mongols,
settled between the Don and the Wolga rivers,
who was said to have professed Christianity, and
to have held out the hope of a diversion from the
North in favour of the cause of that religion
against Islam. The Khan referred to is called by
Rubruquis, Sartach, but in the works of later
French missionaries he is called Gayook Khan.
He was the son of Batoo, at that time great Khan
of the western tribes, and conquered territories of
the Mongols beyond the Caspian Sea. Crossing
the Euxine to the Crimea, Rubruquis found Sartach in the pastures between the Don and Wolga,
which are now occupied by the Cossacks. By
Sartach he was sent on to Batoo, who was then
near the Wolga; and the affair of an expedition
into Syria appearing, even to him, to be beyond
his competency, the monk envoy was sent on to
the Court of Mangoo Khan, at Kara Kurum. He
made the journey in winter, riding relays of horses
along with a Tartar noble, and found no obstruc-
tion except from cold, fatigue, starvation and bad
roads. He remained five months with Mangoo
Khan, and was similarly sent back in the summer.
He writes in his official report of this mission,
made to King Louis, " We came in two months
and ten days from Karakurum to Batoo, and never
saw a town nor so much as the appearance of any

house but graves, except one village, wherein we did not so much as eat bread; nor did we ever rest in these two months and ten days, save one day, because we could not get horses. We went two days, and sometimes three, without taking any other food but cosmos (Kurmis)." The geographical particulars given by Rubruquis are very scanty, but great interest attaches to what he reports of the habits and character of these Khans, and of their courts, and likewise of the religious condition of the Moghuls, or Mongols, in that age. Mangoo Khan was the grandson of Jungeez Khan, who died in the year A.D. 1227, only twenty-six years before the date of this mission. The conquest of China had not yet changed the character and habits of the conquering horde, and we find both Batoo and Mangoo to be the same simple-minded illiterate barbarians that we still read of as occupying the station of Tartar Khans, but not wanting in shrewdness, high-minded feeling, and even dignity.

With respect to religion, Jungeez Khan was the apostle of the most complete toleration. The Mahommedans report that he had the subject discussed in a mosque of Bokhara, and there laid down the principle, that he required only faith in one all-powerful God, leaving all the rest to be supplied by man's free study and judgment. As this was the early creed of Mohammed himself, the Moolavees looked upon him as more than half Mahommedan. But the creed of Jungeez was Boodhism. The very title of Jungeez Khan was given to him by a Kotooktoo, or regenerate Boodh, of great sanctity, after his wars with Tangoot or Tibet, and he was too deep a politician not to use the agency and influence of that extraordinary priesthood to assist him in binding the Tartar, Tibetan and Mongol races in the wonderful association he contrived to establish amongst them, and which subsisted for many generations after his decease.

In the Shensi province a stone tablet was found by the Jesuits, in the seventeenth century, recording the presence of Nestorian Christians in the country, and their success in spreading Christianity, as early as A.D. 636; and there are imperial edicts in its favour of dates between that year and A.D. 782, which are still preserved in the archives and histories of China.

We find also from the report of Father Rubruquis, that Nestorian Christians abounded at the courts and in the territories, as well of Batoo Khan, as of his superior, Mangoo Khan; that they had great influence with many at court, especially of the wives and daughters of these and other chiefs; that they were allowed publicly to profess their

religion, to open chapels, and parade the cross in
public streets and market-places, dressed in ca-
nonical vestments; and that they were especially
called on to administer medicines, and to pray for
sick persons in extremity. Father Rubruquis,
himself, took part in a controversy of these Christians, held with Boodhists and Mohammedans,
in the presence of Mangoo Khan, on matters of
faith; and one cannot read his report without won-
dering at the patience with which these simple-
minded people, and the priests and professors of
their ancient religion submitted to the ill-man-
nered arrogance and pretensions of the intrusive
Christian zealots, who, while proclaiming the mys-
teries of the Trinity, and of the Host, and of holy
water, too frequently insulted those who adhered
to the faith of their fathers, and declared publicly
their books, and those of the Mahommedans, to
be lies, and the believers " vile dogs."

Rubruquis thus reports, in a general way, of the
Lama priesthood he found at the courts of the
Mongol Khans; and we give the extract verbatim,
because it is of importance to show that their
forms and habits have suffered very little change in
the six hundred years since his visit to Mongolia,
and had not their origin in any imitation of
Romish observances, he being the first priest of
that church who is known to have entered the
country.

" All their priests had their heads shaven quite
over, and they are clad in saffron coloured gar-
ments. Being once shaven, they lead an unmarried
life from that time forward, and they live a hundred
or two hundred of them together in one cloister.
Upon the days when they enter into these temples,
they place two long forms therein, and so sitting
upon the said forms, like singing men in a choir,
one half of them directly over against the other,
they have certain books in their hands, which
sometimes they lay down upon the forms; and
their heads are bare as long as they remain in the
temple; and then they read softly to themselves,
not uttering any voice at all. On my coming in
among them, at the time of their superstitious de-
votions, and finding them all sitting mute in a
manner, I attempted several ways to provoke
them to speech, yet could not by any means pos-
sibly. They have with them also, whithersoever
they go, a certain string, with a hundred or two
hundred nutshells thereupon, much like our beads,
which we carry about with us, and they do always
mutter these words, ' *Om mani hactavi*, (*om
mani padme hom*) God, thou knowest,' as one
of them expounded it to me. And so often do
they expect a reward at God's hands as they pro-
nounce these words in remembrance of God."
Again : " I made a visit to their idol temple, and
found certain priests sitting in the outward portico,

and those which I saw seemed by their shaven beards as if they had been our countrymen. They wore certain ornaments upon their heads like mitres made of paper. The priests of the Jugures (Qy? Chakars) use those ornaments wherever they go. They wear always their saffron-coloured jackets, which are very straight-laced, or buttoned from the bosom downwards, after the French fashion, and they have a cloak upon their left shoulder, descending under their right arm, like a deacon carrying a collector's box in time of Lent."

This description corresponds exactly with what one sees at this day in any Boodhist temple of Mongolia, China, Burma, or Siam. Pythagorean silence and abstraction is there the universal rule. The ceremonies and public services on particular occasions, and especially those of the Tibetan monastic establishments, are of a different character, as will hereafter be noticed.

The only further thing to be gathered from Rubruquis is, that the reply of Mangoo Khan to the letter of King Louis, is stated to have been written in the Mongolian language, but in the character of the Jugures or Chakars, which had been introduced by Nestorian Christians, and was derived from the Syrian, but written in lines down the page, commencing from the left. Mongolian is so written at the present day. We wonder if there

is any trace of this letter among the archives of
France ! There are records of older times than
this still subsisting in England, and the letter
which led to the mission of father Rubruquis is
said to be extant.

The next account of these regions obtained by
Europe was furnished through the relation of the
travels of Marco Polo. Two noblemen of the Ve-
netian family of Polo had relations of commerce
and friendship with the Tartar chiefs of the
northern shores of the Euxine, at the very period
of the journey of Rubruquis, above noticed. By
some vicissitudes they were led to Bukhara, at the
time when Alan Khan, better known by the name
of Hulakoo, sent an ambassador to Kublai Khan,
whom he acknowledged as the head of the entire
Tartar and Mongol races. By that ambassador
the Venetians were invited to make the journey
in company. It occupied an entire year, but we
have no record of the line of route followed from
Bokhara. Kublai Khan received them well, and
having kept them some time at his court, sent
them back with letters and a message to the Pope
inviting him to open communications with him.
Some troubles and changes of the papacy prevented
a prompt acknowledgment of this overture; but
at last, in A. D. 1269, as nearly as can be ascertained, the two Polos, Nicolo and Maffei, taking
with them Marco, the young son of the former,

set out on their return, along with a priest, who
soon left them, delivering the Pope's letters into
their hands.   Starting from Acre, on the coast of
Syria, the Polos were three years and a half upon
this journey.   Upon their arrival at Pekin, which
they call Cambala, which is the Tartar name
Khanbaliq, young Marco was taken immediately
into favour, and was for twenty-six years afterwards a nobleman of the great Khan's court, employed in several missions, and other high offices
of state.   He came away at last, in A.D. 1295, in
charge of a princess who was to be married to the
Tartar sovereign of Persia.

The information obtained in this long sojourn
in China and Tartary was committed to writing
by Marco Polo, or from his dictation, during a
captivity he suffered at Genoa, after his return.
It was thus given only from memory, and is often
vague.   But it has been confirmed in most respects
by subsequent travellers.   The route followed, on
the Polos' second journey into China, was up the
Oxus, to its sources, through Budukhshan; whence,
crossing the Pamir table-land to Kotun, they went
across the Hamil or Shamil desert, to Cambala
(Khanbaliq), or Pekin.   The return was by sea to
Singapore, and round Ceylon, to the Persian gulf.
Of Tibet and Mongolia, Marco Polo says little.
His employments seem to have carried him chiefly

into the provinces of China Proper, and other southern countries, the magnitude and population of the cities of which, he details with exaggeration. He dwells also with animation upon the magnificence of the court of Kublai Khan; showing a strange change of habit between him and his predecessor, Mangoo Khan, as described only a few years before by Rubruquis. We find, however, in Marco Polo, continued evidence of the extreme toleration allowed by this race of emperors to all religions, and of the impartiality with which honours were granted to men of every faith. The general who conquered southern China, for instance, is stated to have been a Nestorian Christian, and to have built a church at Nankin for those of his own faith. Marco Polo was himself in high favour, though a Roman Catholic; and Mahommedans also were numerous, and freely employed. It is, indeed, stated to have been the custom of the emperor to send offerings on his birthday to the shrines, and presents to the priests of all religions, on the same principle, it would seem, as was recognised by the Romans when they erected their temple to the gods of lesser nations. This spirit of general toleration did not originate with the Mongol emperors. We learn from the Mahommedan travellers who visited China as early as A.D. 850, that it then prevailed; and that, when Canton was taken and sacked in A.D. 877, by a rebel army, as many as 120,000 Mahommedans, Jews, Christians, and Parsees perished in the sack. This shows that the policy of China in those days allowed the free resort and residence of men of all religions. The same travellers, in common with Rubruquis, relate conferences had with the emperor, or with men in power, on subjects of faith, affording evidence of a spirit of free inquiry into such matters quite consonant with the known principles of Boodhism, which recognises the pursuit of truth by abstraction, and by the free exercise of the powers of the human mind, as the first duty, and only road to perfection. These Mahommedans came to China by sea, and did not penetrate into Tibet or Tartary, which have ever been the head quarters of the religion of Boodh, but they knew of that religion having been derived from India, of its being very ancient, and of its being based on a belief in the transmigration of souls, combined with image worship.

The earliest travels into Tibet Proper which have been transmitted to us, are those of the Jesuit fathers, Grueber and Dorville, who returned from China by that route in A.D. 1661, just four hundred years after Marco Polo's journey westward. They were the first Christians of Europe who are known to have penetrated into the populous parts of Tibet; for Marco Polo's journey was, as we have

stated, to the north-west, by the sources of the
Oxus.* Father Grueber was much struck with
the extraordinary similitude he found, as well in
the doctrine, as in the rituals, of the Boodhists of
Lassa to those of his own Romish faith. He noticed
first, that the dress of Lamas corresponded with
that handed down to us in ancient paintings, as
the dress of the Apostles. 2nd. That the discipline of the monasteries, and of the different orders
of Lamas or priests, bore the same resemblance to
that of the Romish church. 3rd. That the notion
of an incarnation was common to both, so also the
belief in paradise and purgatory. 4th. He remarked that they made suffrages, alms, prayers,
and sacrifices for the dead, like the Roman Catholics. 6th. That they had convents, filled with
monks and friars, to the number of 30,000, near
Lassa, who all made the three vows of poverty,
obedience, and chastity, like Roman monks, be-

---

* Benedict Goez, a Portuguese monk, went from Lahore
by Kabool, to Kashghur, and across the sandy desert, into
China, where he died in A.D. 1607; but his route also was
far north of Tibet. Another Jesuit, Anthony Andrada, passed
through Kumaon to the Manoosa-Rahwa lake, and thence
went on to Rudak, on the western confines of Tibet. His
journey was made in 1624, and is discredited by commen-
tators and geographers, because of his mentioning this lake
as the source of the Ganges and Indus, instead of the Sutlej
There is no doubt, however, that the voyage is genuine,
though we have no details of it.

sides other vows. And 7th, that they had confessors, licensed by the superior Lamas, or bishops; and so empowered to receive confessions, and to impose penances, and give absolution. Besides all this, there was found the practice of using holy water, of singing service in alternation, of praying for the dead, and a perfect similarity in the costumes of the great and superior Lamas to those of the different orders of the Romish hierarchy. These early missionaries, further, were led to conclude, from what they saw and heard, that the ancient books of the Lamas contained traces of the Christian religion, which must, they thought, have been preached in Tibet in the time of the Apostles. We reserve the further discussion of this question, until we have given the more complete and accurate information afforded by recent travellers, who followed very nearly the same route with these missonaries. The sources of our geographical information deserve the first notice.

The map of Tibet, which is given in connection with that of China, was not framed from actual surveys made by the Jesuits employed by the Emperor Kanghi to prepare the latter. They deputed some Lamas, to whom they had imparted the rudiments of the science of surveying, and from their information, filled in that portion. In this state it was published by Du Halde, in the begin-

ning of the eighteenth century, and is to this day
all we have on the subject. The map, therefore,
is on no account to be depended upon. On the
other hand, the few Europeans who have penetrated
into Tibet, with exception to Captain Turner,
Warren Hasting's envoy, tell us only of their difficulties and sufferings, and give very imperfect
notices of the geography of the routes they followed. Fathers Grueber and Dorville crossed China
from Pekin, by Singanfoo to Sining, and reached
the Koko-noor valley, and thence passed into Tibet,
round the sources of the Hwang-ho, and crossing
those of the Yang-tse Kiang river, they came on
from thence to India, through the valley of Nipal
by Katmandu, and Hetounda to Patna, on the
Ganges, where Dorville died. Another missionary,
Père Desideri, started from Goa in November,
1713, and passing through Dehli and Kashmeer
into Baltistan, arrived at Leh, or Ladak, on the
25th June, 1714, and remained there for an entire
year. From thence, he continued his journey, in
the autumn of 1715, to Lassa, by a route of extreme elevation, of which we have no details what-
soever; Desideri, like the rest, only reporting his
own sufferings from the intense cold. The journey
occupied from August 1715, to March 1716; and
the worst part was made in the winter, as seems
to be the case with all, because of the impossi-

bility of crossing the rivers and torrents at other seasons. Desideri found the temporal sovereignty of Lassa in the hands of a Tartar prince (a Sifan), who had recently conquered the country; the Lamas were, however, respected and reverenced, and directed all things spiritual.

After this, a mission of twelve Capuchins was sent into Tibet by Pope Clement XI., at the head of which was a monk named Francis Horace della Penna. It passed through Betia in Behar, to Bhatgaon in Nipal, and thence reached Lassa. In 1732, letters were received in Rome from this mission, after an interval of years, announcing its favourable reception, and soliciting a reinforcement, which was sent in 1738. In 1742, there was published in Rome a very meagre report of the proceedings of this mission, making pretence of great success, and of having brought even the sovereign of the kingdom to acknowledge the truths of Christianity : but stating that he was restrained from proclaiming his conversion by policy, and by a respect for old customs. The mission, which had a branch at Bhatgaon in Nipal, is not further heard of, and no geographical, or other details of interest, have ever been obtained from it.

After these comes, in point of date, the authentic and highly interesting narrative of Captain Turner, who was sent in 1783 by Warren Hastings

on a special political mission to the Grand Lama of
Teeshoo Loomboo. Full particulars of this journey
were published in 1785 in London, with an accurate map of the route; and the book is too well
known to need either citation, or any statement in
abstract of its contents.   We shall hereafter have
occasion to refer to the account it gives of the state
of society and of religion in Tibet. Captain Turner's
route to Lassa was from Rungpoor in Bengal, to
Tassisudon in Bootan, and thence by the Chumu-
lari pass, across the Himalaya, to Teeshoo Loomboo:
— He never went to Lassa. The same route nearly
from Rungpoor was taken by Mr. Manning, who
made the attempt to pass through Tibet into China,
but was sent back from Lassa in 1811.   We are
not aware of any other Europeans having ever penetrated from India into this interesting region ;
but the government of India have received intelligence on several occasions from merchants of
Patna, who trade with Lassa indirectly through
Katmandoo, and its relations with Nipal, have,
more than once, brought the governor-general into
direct communication with the Chinese officers in
Tibet.

It may be convenient to mention in this place
the nature and circumstances of these communications.

In the time of Warren Hastings, the Bootan

chiefs made an incursion into the district of Rung-poor, and the detachment employed in driving back the Booteas penetrated into the lower hills, and took Delamcotta. The Booteas then sued for peace, using the good offices of the Teeshoo Lama for inter-cession, for they are Boodhists, owning the spiritual supremacy of the Tibetan Lamas. Favourable terms were given to them, and Delamcotta was restored. The missions, first of Mr. Bogle, and afterwards of Captain Turner, to Teeshoo-loomboo had their origin in this petty war. The British power, it is to be observed, was not then viewed with the same suspicion as at present, either by Tibetans or by Chinese, nor was the authority of China so firmly established in Tibet.

In 1792, the Goorkhas having mastered the whole of the valley of Nipal, and of the hill country from Sikhim to the Gogra, a party of them crossed the Himalaya, and appeared suddenly before Teeshoo Loomboo. The Lama and priests hastily evacuated their convents, and fled to Lassa, and the place was plundered by the Goorkhas, who retired immediately with their booty. The Tibetans applied to China for aid, and an army was collected for the punishment of this act of unprovoked outrage. The Goorkhas met them at Tingri Mydan, and the two armies were for some time in presence, but the Chinese made at last a general attack, and the Nipalese were defeated. The Chinese general, following up his victory, took the frontier post of Nipal, called Koti, and showed a disposition further to penetrate into the southern hills. Captain Kirkpatrick was at this time resident at Katmandoo, on the part of Lord Cornwallis, governor-general of India. His instructions were, studiously to avoid anything like interference in the quarrel with Tibet; but to hold the language of reprobation and displeasure in respect to this unprovoked act of the Goorkha court. The consequence was, that despairing of aid from us, the Goorkhas submitted unconditionally to the Chinese commander, who imposed a tribute and triennial mission to Pekin, besides restitution of all the booty taken at Teeshoo Loomboo, and took hostages for the performance of these stipulations. The Raja of Sikhim was at the same time taken under Chinese protection, so as to prevent the extension of Goorkha conquest eastward. This is the state with which we have recently had a quarrel consequently upon the detention of Dr. Campbell, our agent at Darjeeling, while upon an excursion beyond the limits of that station, which excited Chinese jealousy, and was so resented by the intervention of the local authorities, most probably at their instance or suggestion.

Checked towards the East by these events, the Goorkhas extended their dominion westward, subjugating Kumaon, Sirinugur, and all the hill country to the Sutlej. Their restless rapacity could not be restrained from plundering and encroaching upon British subjects, and rajas within the British frontier. This brought on the Nipal war of 1814—16, which terminated in the British conquest of Kumaon, and of all the western hills, and in the cession of that territory to the British by a formal treaty, which was signed and delivered to General Ochterlony, on the 4th March, 1816. It is under the stipulations of this treaty that we have now a permanent resident stationed at Katmandoo.

The Chinese viewed, with great jealousy, the establishment of a British political officer at the court of one of their tributaries, for the Nipal Raja had continued since 1792 to send the triennial mission, with presents, to Pekin, in acknowledgment of fealty. In September, 1816, the court of Pekin sent a special commissioner, with such troops as could be collected, to call their feudatory to account for his proceedings. A mission of explanation was accordingly sent from Katmandoo, which was rated soundly by the Chinese commissioner, whose name was Choong Chang, for having brought war upon their country by wanton aggressions and acts of violence, and for having represented the British object in the war

to be to obtain command of the passes into Tibet.
To the Governor-General of India, Choong Chang
wrote as follows :—

"His Imperial Majesty, who, by God's blessing,
is well informed of the conduct and proceedings
of all mankind, reflecting on the good faith and
wisdom of the English, and the firm friendship
and constant commercial intercourse which has
so long subsisted between the two nations, never
placed any reliance on the calumnious imputations
put forward by the Goorkha Raja," &c. &c. "You
mention that you have stationed an envoy in
Nipal. This is a matter of no consequence; but,
as the raja from his youth and inexperience, and
from the novelty of the thing, has imbibed sus-
picions, if you would, out of kindness to us, and
in consideration of the ties of friendship subsisting,
withdraw your envoy. It would be better; and
we should feel inexpressibly gratified for the consideration shown to our wishes." To this, the
Marquis of Hastings replied, that if the Chinese
government would send a high officer to Nipal,
through whom we might seek redress, in case of
future injuries and aggressions, we might then
dispense with the presence of an envoy at Katmandoo: otherwise there seemed no alternative
but to keep him there, to give and receive expla-
nations, as the best and only way of preventing

differences hereafter. To this the court of China
replied, after a long interval, in these words :—
" Be it known to you, that the Goorkha Raja has
long been a faithful tributary of the Chinese government, and refers himself to it whenever occasion requires. There is, therefore, no need of
deputing thither any one from this empire. Besides, by the grace of God, His Majesty, possessing
the sovereignty of the whole kingdom of China,
and other countries, does not enter the city of any
one without cause. If it so happen that his victorious forces take the field, in such case, after
punishing the refractory, he, in his royal clemency,
restores the transgressor to his throne. We have
not thought it our duty to represent this matter
to the throne, as it is opposed to the customs of
this empire. The merchants who frequent the
port of Canton, can inform your lordship of our
customs. *For the future, a proposition so contrary
to usage, should not be introduced into a friendly
dispatch.*" With this display of humour the correspondence closed. It is to be remarked as singular, that Tibet is never once referred to by the
Chinese officers. The affair is treated as one concerning China and its tributary, Nipal, and none
other. In the time of Warren Hastings, when
we were embroiled with Bootan, under circumstances not dissimilar, it was the Teeshoo Lama

who interceded, and with whom we had relations in consequence. The Emperor of China was then only the friend and patron of the Lamas of Tibet, but in 1816 their political existence was absolutely ignored. This change seems to have resulted from the resort to Chinese military aid, in order to repel the Nipalese incursion of 1792.

Tibet thus rested in its sleep of isolation, shut out from European travellers and unheard of in the annals of the world's history, until the Sikh conquest of Ladak and Balti, on its western frontier, disturbed in some measure its repose. Zorawur Singh, the Sikh general, who commanded the expedition, sent from Kashmeer by Goolab Singh in 1839, after taking Ladak and Iskardo, marched up the valley of the Indus into Gnari, a province of Tibet, and captured Gurtokh, its capital. His force was inconsiderable, and he wrote in vain for supplies and reinforcements. They were not easily furnished across the many intervening ranges of snow-capped mountains. Winter was now approaching, and Zorawur Singh fortified for himself a cantonment near Gurtokh, when a Chinese and Tibetan force surrounded him and cut off his supplies. His detachment was thus overpowered and himself slain. About 120 miserable Sikh fugitives found their way, half frozen, across the Niti Pass, into the British province of Kumaon,

and told the tale. This occurred in the winter of
1842, at the very time when the British force of
Kabool was similarly overpowered by the Afghans.
The Chinese and Tibetans did not follow up their
victory, and made no use of it to extend their
frontier towards Ladak. The Sikhs, therefore,
soon recovered, and have since maintained, their
possession of the valleys as well of the Indus, up
to Debrung, as of the entire Shayuk river. When
the Sikh war with the British closed in the establishment of our ascendancy in the Punjab, and in
the permanent assignment of Kashmeer and its
tributaries to Raja Goolab Singh, British officers
were sent to ascertain and settle the frontier line
of the territory so committed to his management,
where it met that of territory subject to Tibet or
China. This duty was executed by Lieutenant
Strachey, whose mission has furnished much
geographical information and many scientific details respecting the elevated regions he visited
beyond the Himalaya, and in which these two
rivers have their sources.

While, however, Tibet has been thus hermeti-
cally sealed against us on the side of India, two
French missionaries have succeeded in effecting a
passage into it, and in reaching its capital, Lassa,
from the north-east. They came from the Koko
Noor by the same route that had been followed by

fathers Grueber and Dorville, two centuries before,
and one of them, Monsieur Huc, has recently
published in two volumes, in French, a full account
of the incidents of this journey. It is the conviction of the trustworthiness of the information contained in these volumes, and the desire to make
it more extensively known to the British public,
and especially to those Englishmen whose occupa-
tions abroad give value to authentic details regarding the habits, religion and geography of these
little known regions, that we have been led to
make this compilation and to compress the substance of M. Huc's work into the following pages.

Every one has heard of the mission established
at Pekin under French Jesuits. The founder of it
was Pere Ricci, who went from Macaointo the interior of China, in A.D. 1585, and established himself
in the first instance at Nankin. He was a good
mathematician, and making himself master of the
Chinese language, published some maps of the
world in Chinese; and gave lessons and instructions generally in European sciences. He thus
acquired in that country a high reputation for
learning, and commenced circulating tracts upon
religion, and upon the immortality of the soul, and
a future state. Sometimes persecuted, and sometimes applauded and followed, he removed, after a
few years, from Nankin to Pekin, where he was well

received; and his doctrines made an impression
on some nobles of the court. He lived there
for many years, the recognised head of several
missionary establishments, located in different
parts of China, making many converts, and respected by all until his death, which occurred at
the age of fifty-seven, in the year 1610. The
Ming dynasty was at this period in its decadence.
Chun-chi, the Manchoo Tartar completed its fall
in 1644. During these convulsions the French
Jesuits met with varied fortune; but Chun-Chi,
upon his assumption of the imperial dignity, in the
year stated, called Father Schall, the successor of
Father Ricci, to his court at Pekin, and received
him there with great distinction, nominating him
president of the tribunal of mathematics, and
giving him the *entrée* to his own presence at all
times, with other favours. Upon Chun-Chi's death,
at an advanced age, in A.D. 1662, his successor,
Kang-hi, was only eight years old, and during his
minority the Jesuits and their converts were proscribed and persecuted by the Chinese tribunals.
Father Adam Schall died in prison during these
persecutions, under sentence of death, and the
Jesuit missions were for a time broken up. But
when Kang-hi came to his majority, and took into
his own hands the reins of power, he caused the
sentence of condemnation passed against Adam

c

Schall to be reversed, and received the Jesuits
again into favour. A maternal uncle of the Emperor declared himself a convert in A.D. 1672, and
was publicly baptized; others followed, and fresh
missions were, at this period, established in different parts of China, where the religion spread
capidly. Father Verbien, the successor of Adam
Schall, wrote now to the Pope, to ask for assist-
ance in the work of conversion; and further missions of Dominicans, Franciscans, and Augustins,
were despatched from Rome, to carry out the
views and realize the high expectations then en-
tertained. Father Verbien died unfortunately
just at the time when these reinforcements arrived, and a schism then arose between the Jesuits
and the Dominicans, as to the propriety of allowing Chinese converts to continue the rites and
observances practised universally by that nation in
honour of parents and ancestors. The Jesuits
were for yielding this, and for not regarding the
reverence so paid to ancestry in the light of an ido-
latrous worship inconsistent with the Christian
notion of the Divine nature, as the sole object of
adoration and prayer. Not so the Dominicans;
and this schism not only divided and paralyzed
the action of the missions in China, but for nearly
a century it was debated all over Europe, and
was carried even to the papal authority for final de-

cision. After many rescripts, and several fruitless attempts to reconcile differences and avoid giving a final judgment, Clement XI. at last, in 1710, declared finally against yielding any indulgence to Chinese usage in the matter of reverence to parents and ancestors, and sent out a Legate Cardinal, a M. de Tournon, to enforce this decision, in 1715.

Kang-hi, the Chinese Emperor, had in the mean time taken the Jesuits into great favour. He employed them in rectifying his calendar, and in surveying and mapping his dominions, and in teaching his subjects to cast cannon and other useful arts, and but for this schism magnificent results might have followed. But when he heard of the Pope's decision in favour of the Dominicans, he took a decided part for the maintenance of the institutions and usages of his own subjects. He treated the Legate, M. de Tournon, with harshness, and ordered him back to Canton immediately he learned that he was the bearer of orders from the Pope, to disallow parental reverence, and the usual observances; and Christianity was exhibited and proclaimed to the Chinese, as a false and seditious conspiracy to overturn the laws and institutions of the empire, and to set sons against fathers, and wives against husbands. It is on this ground that the preaching and proclaiming of Christianity

c 2

is to this day proscribed in China. All the persecutions of the eighteenth century had their origin
in the conviction, that the defence and maintenance
of the ancient laws in favour of the parental authority required an overt action against doctrines quite
repugnant to these usages and observances, and
which substituted the priest for the parent in
every family.

But Kanghi, though he took this strong part
against the papal decree in support of the Dominicans, continued to favour the Jesuits of his court,
whose scientific services he still needed. He died
in 1722, after a prosperous reign of sixty years.
Yong-Ching, who succeeded him, encouraged the
tribunals in their persecution of the converts to
Christianity, and even banished from court the
Jesuits, and several members of his own family,
who favoured the new religion.

Kien-long, who succeeded to the throne in
1735, and who reigned, like Kang-hi, for sixty
years, recalled his Christian relatives from exile,
and seemed at first favourably disposed to the
Jesuit missions; but upon a representation from
his high officers, he at last passed an edict for the
expulsion of all priests and missionaries. The
Jesuits were, at this period, proscribed in Europe
also, and the mission they had established in
China languished in consequence, and fell into in-

action; and thus, for want of due support to keep alive the zeal both of professors and preachers the hope of extensively spreading Christianity in China yielded to the severity with which the edicts against preaching its doctrines were carried into execution. Some Jesuits appear, however, to have been permitted to maintain a small establishment at Pekin, for the purpose of assisting in the preparation of the annual almanacks; but they were restricted from preaching, and not allowed to travel, or to communicate freely with strangers, and were scarcely recognised. The Emperor, Kia-King, who ascended the throne in 1799, completed the destruction of the hopes of the propagandists, and driving the last remains of the French mission out of Pekin, renewed the persecution of converts with greater rigour.

In China Proper, there are tribunals with a strict police, and a machinery of local administration, that made it nearly impossible for converts to Christianity to evade the law and escape punishment. They were everywhere discovered and plundered; and if they would not consent to renounce the new faith, their lives even were in danger. But the influence of Chinese laws, and of the civil power for the execution of edicts is very different beyond the Great Wall. In Mongolia, called by the Chinese the Land of Herbs, the Tartar tribes retain

their own laws and forms of government. Each
Khan, or Tao-tse tributary, rules his own tribe, and
the simple habits of the men of the desert make
that rule very light and easy. The Chinese, taking
advantage of this simplicity, emigrate largely from
China, and settle in the valleys of Mongolia, where-
ever they can find a soil that will repay cultivation. They appear to settle down as separate and
nearly independent communities, under elected
chiefs or captains, and whether dealing with the
chief of a tribe, or with individuals, contrive generally to get the better, displacing the nomade population, and establishing their own usages and
modes of life. The persecution of Christian converts by the Chinese authorities, led many of them
to become emigrants to Mongolia. Several settle-
ments were accordingly formed by them in the
valleys of the southern feeders of the river Amour,
or Sagalien, about one hundred miles due north
of Pekin. In the days of the Republic, and of
the Empire in France, little heed was taken of the
relations of the ancient French Church with these
people; but upon the restoration of the Bourbons
they became the subject of inquiry, and zealous men
of the religious orders were not wanting to under-
take the mission of reclaiming and bringing again
within that Church the scattered flock of its persecuted proselytes. In the Ooniot district of

" the Land of Herbs," there is a valley called that
of " the Black Waters," whither many of the
Chinese converts had retired. There an establishment was formed under Lazarist missionaries
from Paris, which unobtrusively following its vo-
cation, gathered together a considerable congregation of these converts, and brought many Mon-
golians also to accept the Christian creed. Hear·
ing of their success, the Roman Pontiff, in 1842,
appointed the head of this mission, who resided
at Siwang, to be his vicar-apostolic in Mongolia.
Excited by this to fresh efforts, these Lazarist
missionaries conceived the design of exploring the
desert further, and of penetrating even into Tibet,
with a view to the establishment there of a subor-
dinate mission. Two members of the brotherhood,
Messrs. Gabet and Huc, were selected by the
vicar-apostlic for this adventurous duty; and the
account, recently published by the latter, of the
circumstances and events of their journey, and of
its toils and dangers, furnishes proof abundant of
the judicious selection made, and of the high qua-
lifications for the undertaking possessed by both
missionaries. In the dress and character of
Tibetan Lamas, attended by a single servant, a
man of a half-civilised race from the vicinity of
the Koko-noor, who had been brought to profess
Christianity, these two French gentlemen started

from the "Valley of Black Waters," north of Pekin,
to live for years the life of Tartars of the desert;
subsisting on their meagre fare, and enduring all
their hardships and privations; cherished and
supported during their severe trials by the high
aim of their sacred calling, and by their devotion
to the faith they desired to spread. They took the
line of the great wall of China, but kept generally
on the desert side of it, and so followed up the
Hoang-Ho, or Yellow River, till they reached and
rounded its sources. Wintering in the valley of
the Koko-noor, Salt Lake, they next year crossed
the yet more mighty Yang-tse-Kiang, or Blue
River, and so reached the Snowy Mountains and
high table-lands of Tibet, which separate the waters
of China from those of India. Passing these in
the midst of winter, they penetrated at last to
the city of Lassa, where they were well received by
the Tibetan authorities. There it was their design to have established a separate mission under
the Mongolian vicar-apostolic; but the Chinese
envoy at Lassa, the same Ke-Shin, who met the
British admiral at the mouth of the Pichelee, in
1840, and who negotiated the first treaty with
Mr. Elliot afterwards at Canton, laid his veto on
the scheme, and sent the two missionaries back
into China, by a route, hitherto, so far as we
know, quite unexplored by any European. They

passed among the mountains north of Bootan and Ava, and so made their way due east to the plains of " the Central Flowery Land," where these are watered by the Yang-tse-Kiang, in its full magnificence. It is of this journey, and of its hardships, perils and privations, exceeding perhaps those ever endured by travellers who lived to tell the tale, that M. Huc has given us his recollections. The travellers could keep no journal; their lives would have been forfeited, if they had been seen to take notes, or to make sketches of what they saw and heard. It is on this account, that we find a lamentable deficiency of dates, distances, and of other particulars of the kind that one usually looks for in books of travels. Nevertheless, there is in the volumes an aggregate of intelligence, and a fund of characteristic traits, and welltold anecdotes, bearing intrinsically the stamp of truth, and that gives to them a value and an interest far exceeding those of ordinary books of the kind, and sufficient fully to compensate the reader for the want of the scientific details of a Humboldt and a Pallas. But what is in our eyes by far the most important part of these recollections of M. Huc, is the details we find there of the monastic and academic institutions of Tartary and Tibet, and of the studies, habits, and discipline of the several classes of Lamas. The two

missionaries lived for months together in lamaserais, or convents, in the valley of the Koko-
noor, Salt Lake, associating daily with Lamas of
all degrees, and mixing in their studies. Their
information on these subjects, therefore, is not
that of mere passing travellers; and their observations on the working of the Boodhist monastic
system, in its influence on the people, and in its
relations with the Manchoo Government of China,
derive additional value from their own connection
with similar institutions of Europe.

But we trespass on the patience of our readers
by this preface. They will be impatient for a
summary of the real contents of the volumes. To
this, therefore, we hasten.

In preparation for the journey, the missionaries
employed a Mongol convert to procure camels
from the borders of Tibet. They had nearly despaired of the arrival of these animals, owing to
the time that had elapsed since they heard of
their dispatch, and had in consequence made
arrangements for their own departure in a waggon
of the country, when the camels made their appearance, under their faithful conductor, a Chiaour
of Northern Tibet, named Sambda-Chamba, who
had been brought up as a Lama before his conversion, and still wore the dress. The caravan
was then arranged, and commenced its march in

the following order :—The Tibetan led, mounted on
a black mule, and drawing after him a string of
two camels, bearing a tent and the baggage.
M. Gabet rode next upon a dromedary, and M. Huc
brought up the rear, mounted on a white horse.
These, with a watch-dog, formed the entire train
that started for a journey of five-and-twenty degrees of longitude and ten of latitude, across the
unknown elevated regions of central Asia. Before
starting, the missionaries had to change their costume. Amongst their Chinese converts, they had
dressed habitually in the secular habit of China,
wearing the long tail, so inestimably prized by all
of this nation. For the journey, they shaved their
heads, and assumed the same dress as their conductor, Sambda Chamba, which was the secular
habit of a Tibetan Lama. This was essential for
the character the travellers intended to bear, which
was that of Lamas of the west, come to inquire
into the doctrines and ritual of Tibet, the holy
ground of the Boodhist religion. As laymen
(called by Tibetans, black men), it would have
been impossible for them to have talked of religion, or to have shown any acquaintance with
its doctrines or ritual, but as secular Lamas the
enquiry was both natural and praiseworthy. The
missionaries, though they carried a tent, were
glad to put up at the hotels of the country, where

there were any, as was ordinarily the case, within
the frontiers of China Proper. There they found
always a hot meal, and a *kang*, or elevated dais,
so contrived as to be heated by the same fire that
served to boil the caldron that cooked their din-
ners. The guests sit cross-legged upon the kang
for their meal, and spread their beds afterwards
in rows, with their feet towards one other, and so
in the severest winter our travellers contrived to
sleep with some comfort. In the tent there was
no such security from the cold, and sometimes
they had the greatest difficulty in even lighting a
fire, which, at the best, was but of argols or dung-
fuel.

Yan-pa-ool was the direct town from which the
start was made. Thence, after three hours of laborious ascent, the caravan reached the table-land
of the Sain-oula Mountains, in which the Chara
Mooren, a large tributary of the Amour or Sagalien,
has its sources. On this table-land, the travellers
began their experience of the hardships of Tartar
travel. After pitching their tent, they had to collect the argols, or dung, left by the camels and
other animals of preceding caravans, which ordinarily was the only fuel available throughout the
whole of their long journey. With this fuel, when
they had made their pot to boil, they heated some
" *Kwamin*," a kind of vermicelli, prepared for the

purpose, which, with a slice of bacon added, when procurable, formed the whole of their luxurious meal at the commencement of the journey. As they proceeded, this meal was reduced to "Tsamba," a decoction of brick-tea,* and meal mixed up with a little butter. For more than an entire year, these French missionaries had very rarely a superior meal to such as we have above described, and never better beds than their skin cloaks spread upon the ground. Hear this, ye travellers by rail and steam-boat! who grumble if your dinner of three courses be not served in ten minutes, and who find nothing but discomfort in the princely hotels of the Rhine and of the high roads of Europe!

On the table-land of the Sainoolla, the travellers crossed part of the hunting ground of Jeho-ool, which they describe as of surpassing beauty and richness. The descent to the south-west brought them to the district of Jeshekten (Gechekten), a fertile country, in which Chinese industry and chicanery are encroaching largely on the pastoral habits, and on the properties of the Mongols. In this district, as well as in that of the Ooniots, left by the missionaries on the other side of the Sain-

* The tea of Tartary is formed into bricks by compression of the leaves, and is very coarse and inferior to that sold by the Chinese for the European market.

oola range, gold is procured in abundance.   It
exists in mines; and there is a class of men among
the Chinese, who possess, or pretend to, the power
of discovering from the soil and vegetation where
this metal is to be found.   Upon a discovery being
declared by one of these, parties of vagabonds
gather about him, who, with their head-quarters
at the mine, commit excesses far exceeding those
of California, and subsist by plundering the entire
neighbourhood.   M. Huc tells a story of a body
of miners, who so settled in the Ooniot country to
the number of 12,000, and for two years were the
terror of the vicinity.   At last, a Mongol princess
passing near the mine, was plundered of her jewels,
which induced the Ooniot chieftain to collect his
horde for vengeance.   The Chinese were overpowered and massacred without mercy, and many
of them taking refuge in their mine, the mouth
was blocked up, and they perished miserably.   This,
be it observed, was not 200 miles from the capital,
and shows how little real authority the Chinese
government possesses over the free hordes of
Mongolia; but of that, more presently.   From
Jeshekten, the travellers passed into the district of
the eight banners of Chakars, the same nation
apparently that Father Rubruquis calls Jugures.
There, meeting some Tartars in search of stray
horses, they were much importuned to cast a

horoscope to determine in what direction the lost
animals would be found. Their servant wondered
at their refusal, and told how well he had fared
heretofore by acceding to such requests. Divina-
tion, it seems, is one of the recognised sources of
a Lama's livelihood.

In the Chakar district, they came to the city of
Tolo-Noor (seven lakes) called by Chinese "Lama
Mias," by Mongols "Nadan Omo," by Tibetans
" Sat Doon." On the French map the place bears
the name of " Naiman Soomè." What can a
geographer do with such a nomenclature? This
city, like most of those of China, has no munici-
pality, no police, no drainage, no pavement, no
lights. The passage through its streets is, in consequence, perilous as well as difficult, from obstruc-
tions of all kinds; if a wheel carriage upsets, a
mob plunders it with impunity, and camels and
other laden animals are frequently disabled in the
muddy quagmires, and similarly at once rifled.
Still, the city is a great mart of the commerce of
Tartary, as well with Northern China as with
Kiakhta. There are foundries in Tolo-Noor for
casting brass and iron statues, bells and metal
utensils of all kinds, and the missionaries witnessed the dispatch to Tibet of a statue of Boodh,
cast in pieces, and laden upon eighty-four camels.
They availed themselves of the opportunity of their

visit to this mart, to have a Christ cast in bronze
after a French model, and M. Huc bears testimony
to the high state of art of the Chinese, declaring
that it was impossible to distinguish the copy from
the original.

On the 1st of October, 1844, one of the very
few dates of our calendar given by M. Huc, the
missionaries left Tolo-Noor. Their camels passed
through the slippery and deep mire of the streets
with extreme difficulty. But they were no sooner
beyond the suburbs, than they entered upon the
sands of the great Tartar desert. After a fatiguing
day's march, they encamped at a mineral spring
of very nauseous water, but finding wood fuel,
made a luxurious meal. The next day they fell
in with the suite of a princess of the royal race of
Jungeez Khan, of the Khalkhas tribe, who was
travelling upon a pilgrimage to the famous Boodhist monastery of the five towers in the province
of Shense. They left the princess, after a cour-
teous interchange of civilities, and pushed on until
overtaken by a storm of wind and rain, in the
midst of which they vainly endeavoured to set up
their tent and light their fire. They were relieved
by some hospitable Mongols, who saw their distress. One of these proved to be a soldier, not
long returned from the war with the English. He
stated the order of service in the Chinese empire

to be that "first the Chinese militia are sent against an invading enemy. Next the banner of the Solo hordes is raised. After them the Chakar tribes are called out." "Were all the Chakars called out on this occasion?" asked the missionaries. "Yes," said the soldier, "all." "At first, little was thought of the war, and it was said the Chakars will not be required; but the Chinese militia could do nothing. The Solo troops marched, but the heat of the South destroyed them. Then came the Emperor's order into our country; every one immediately furbished his arms and prepared for the campaign. For six generations we had not been called upon, but the Emperor, who gave us this fine country, now required our services. We felt we must answer the call. The eight banners were gathered, and we marched to Pekin. Thence they sent us to Tien-Tsin-vei, where we were in camp for three months." "Did you ever see the enemy and meet them in battle?" "No! he dared not show himself. The Chinese told us we were marching to certain death; that the enemy were sea monsters, hiding themselves under water, and coming out when not expected, to discharge fiery water melons (bombs and shells), that before one could bend a bow against them, they disappeared again under water, like frogs. Us, too, they thought to frighten with such stories.

But we cared not. The Grand Lama had been
consulted and had assured us of a prosperous
issue. We had a Lama acquainted with medicine
attached to each (Chounda) company, and why
should we fear? But the enemy, when they heard
of our approach, were alarmed and sued for peace;
and our holy master (the Emperor) acceded to
their request out of compassion, so we returned
without meeting him." This Mongol soldier left
the missionaries before they could further satisfy
their curiosity about the events of the war.

The Chakar country is bounded on the east by
Jeshekten, on the west by Tourmet, and by the
Sooniot district on the north, and is said to be a
hundred and fifty leagues long, by a hundred
broad. The district was assigned to the eight
banners of the Chakar horde as a barrier against
the Khalkhas, which, as being the tribe of Jungeez Khan, the Manchoos view with great jealousy,
as well because of its ancient glories, as of the
aspirations which the descendants of this mighty
conqueror still delight to entertain. A Chakar
cannot sell his assigned land to other than a
Chakar. A Chinese purchaser is at once ejected.
The Chakars are guardians of the imperial stud
and draw considerable emoluments from the frauds
which the trust enables them to perpetrate.

From the Chakar country, the missionaries passed

to Chaborté (the swamp), which they reached on the day of the Yue-ping (moon cake) festival. This festival is of great antiquity; but, since the year 1368, it has been kept by the Chinese with particular honour; for in that year, a Sicilian vesper was prepared secretly against the Tartars, and the announcement of the hour of rising was circulated in the cakes of the festival. This perversion of the rites of the day has, however, been forgotten in the lapse of years, and Mongols now join with the Chinese in its celebration. The missionaries were invited by a Mongol to partake of the festivities, and with very questionable good breeding reminded the host of the massacre of his ancestors, to which the festival had contributed; but this did not affect the cordiality of their reception. They were presented with brother Benjamin's slices of the fat of monstrous sheep's-tails, a great delicacy, though far beyond their digestive powers. They divided and distributed the tit-bits among the guests, and then fared heartily on the flesh. A Toolholos sang in this assembly several national songs commemorative of the glory of the Mongols, and amongst them, the spirited lament for Tymoor, so exciting to a Tartar. He gave them but half-an-hour, and then went his round to other households, singing at each for a large gratuity, proportioned to his skill. After a stay of two days, to

replenish their stores with fresh purchases, they
prepared for a start from Shaborté, but found their
mule and horse missing. The friendly Mongols
undertook the search, and soon recovered them.
The missionaries then took the route to Koko
Khoton, or " the blue city." On the third day of
their march, they fell in with a deserted city, the
walls of which they found entire, and the houses
half buried in sand and earth. The place had the
appearance of having been so deserted for centuries,
and no Tartar could furnish information either of
the time or cause of the desertion. M. Huc says
that the desert abounds in such remains of all
dimensions. He assigned to them a date coeval
with the expulsion of the Mongols from China,
and ascribed them to the severities of Young-ho,
an early sovereign of the Ming dynasty, who endeavoured to annihilate the Tartars. We should
rather suspect some failure of water to be the cause
of the desertion of these localities, for if the site
were favourable, they would assuredly have been
soon re-peopled. Near this ruined city, the travellers crossed the great southern road from Kiakta,
by which the Russian missions are ordinarily conducted to Pekin.

Two more days carried the travellers into the
kingdom of Efé, a part of the ancient territory of
the Khalkhas, lost by them during the wars which

preceded the establishment of the present dynasty. The early sovereigns of Manchoo race gave this tract to the Chakars ; but it was taken again from the eight banners of this nation, to be given by Kienlong as dower of a princess of the imperial family, married by him to a prince of the ancient race of Jungeez.

The Mongols of Efé are famous for their skill as wrestlers, and from infancy are continually training themselves. They take pride in carrying off the prizes in the annual contests held at many places, one of which occurred when M: Timkouski was at Oorga, and he certifies to the skill of this tribe.

On the 22nd day of the 8th moon, after passing out of Efé, the travellers crossed a range of hills on the road to the Chorchi Lamaserai, of one of the inmates of which they had heretofore made a convert, while he taught them the Mongol language. There are 200 Lamas on the Chorchi establishment, which, being a favourite of the Emperor's, has been richly endowed. But these institutions rarely owe their origin to imperial bounty. When it is proposed to build one, a number of Lamas start in all directions to collect subscriptions from the pious. Wherever they go, they are hospitably received, and rarely fail to make a large collection, which, on their return, is devoted to the erection of suitable buildings of brick or stone :

Round these again, the pious further build temples
and tombs, by which means the desert is soon converted into the appearance of a city. The Lamas
are themselves the sculptors and painters, and frequently the artificers also in the construction of
these edifices. The principal Lamaserai of all
Mongolia is that of the Great Kouren (the Oorga
Kooren, of Tim-kouski), situated in the country
of the Khalkas, on the banks of the Toula river,
and standing on the edge of the great forest that
stretches northward into Siberia. To the south, lies
the desert of a month's journey. It, stands, however, in a pleasant valley, amid mountains near the
source of the Toula, which river falls into the great
Baikal lake. There are 30,000 Lamas, under
several heads, at Oorga; their chief is the Geesoo-
Tamba, a regenerated Boodh, of great sanctity.
There has, of course, risen a large city and mart of
commerce in the immediate vicinity of the convent,
and it is the head quarters of Mongolia, having
been the capital of the princes of the family of
Jungeez Khan, before their conquest of China.
Tea-bricks are here the measures of value, an ounce
of silver representing five tea-bricks. There are
Chinese mandarins at Grand Kouren, ostensibly to
preserve the peace amongst the Chinese merchants,
—but, in reality, to act as spies on the Geesoo-
Tamba, whose influence and power are very much

dreaded at Pekin. In 1839, the Geesoo-Tamba
announced a visit to the court of Pekin, which was
the cause of great alarm. His retinue was ordered
to be reduced to 3,000 Lamas, and the three petty
sovereigns of Oorga, descended from Jungeez, were
forbidden to accompany him. Still, as this hierarch
marched through Mongolia, he was received everywhere with extraordinary honours. Supplies were
provided, and wells dug at the resting-places of his
route, and the Tartars thronged from all parts to
meet and worship him. At the Great Wall, half
his small retinue was further stopped, still his presence gave great inquietude to the imperial government, and he was soon dispatched from the capital,
to visit the Lamaserai of the Five Towers, and the
Blue City. He died on his way home, the victim,
it was said, of imperial jealousy; for it was strongly
suspected that he received at Pekin a slow poison.
It is very much the custom for these sanctified persons to die, before they reach the seats of their
spiritual supremacy, on their return. Perhaps the
Chinese know they return dissatisfied in their
hearts, if not disgusted, with the result of their
visit to Pekin; and fearing, therefore, to leave this
feeling rankling in the breast of persons of such
extensive influence, prefer to promote a regeneration, and to take the opportunity of professing
reverence and regret, and the most profound per-

sonal attachment, in a long obituary notice in the
Pekin Gazette.

In 1844, the Geesoo Tamba was regenerated in
Tibet, and our missionaries met in the Koko-noor
valley the mission of Khalkas Tartars, which was
proceeding to bring him from thence to the Grand
Kooren monastery. In Mongolia, besides the
Grand Kooren monastery at Oorga, there are the
Mingan Lamari Kooren, i.e., the thousand Lama
monastery, also that of Koko Khoton, " the Blue
City," and the Polou-noor, and Jeho-ool, Lama-
serais, in all of which, the Lamas have both civil
and criminal jurisdiction. Within the wall of
China there are the monasteries of Pekin, of the
Five Towers, and of Shensi, all of the same high
rank and privileges.

From Chorchi, the missionaries entered again
the territory of the Chakars. They were now in the
lands of the Red Banner of that nation. From
thence, after several days march, they passed into
Western Tourmet. The eastern district of that
name lies on the other side of the Chakar territory. In the western district Chinese habits have
the ascendancy, and agriculture is extending.
Everything seemed here prosperous, and trees even
had been planted on the road-side. Three days
march in Western Tourmet brought the travellers
to the " Blue City "—Koko-Khoton, as it is called

in Mongolian—Kui-hwa-chen in Chinese. There
are two cities close to one another, the old and the
new; the new being the Tartar, or military establishment, built by Kang-hi, with magnificent
walls. Here the missionaries found a force of
10,000 men, under a Kiang-kian. The soldiers were
originally Manchoo Tartars, but had nearly forgotten the Manchoo language. The missionaries
remarked, indeed, that generally, in China as well
as in Mongolia, the Manchoos had lost their na-
tionality as the result of their ascendancy. A
Manchoo is under obligation to enrol himself under
some banner, and, failing to do so, loses his privileges. Many neglect to enrol themselves volun-
tarily in order to avoid the conscription. The
Sifo and Solon are the highest tribes of Manchoos.
These are proud of their position and history, but
without much cause on the ground of antiquity or
of civilization, for the Manchoos had no written
character until 1641, nor was the language reduced to rule, and arranged in dictionaries and
grammars, until the reign of Kien Long, that is
towards the end of the eighteenth century. Mok-
den is the native capital of the Manchoos. The
Emperor has a palace there, and it is a handsome
city, one quarter of which is appropriated to the
" Yellow Belts," that is, to the members of the Imperial family. In the northern districts, near the

D

Sagalien, a very productive kind of cotton is said to grow, yielding, says M. Huc, in a square of fifteen feet, French, as much as two thousand pounds of cotton.

Losing themselves in the muddy streets of Koko-Khoton, the travellers were exposed to the villany of a sharper, who reckoned upon *selling* them as Tartar simpletons, but they extricated themselves adroitly by taking refuge in the very respectable Chinese hotel of "three perfections." Here established, they prepared for the coming winter by the purchase of sheep-skin cloaks and clothing. There is no coined money in China, except the brass pieces with a hole in the centre, of which every one will have seen specimens. Silver is sold by the weight, and an ounce is the equivalent of from 1700 to 1800 of these brass coins, which are called sapeks by the Europeans, by the Chinese Tien, and by Tartars Deboy. In taking change for some ounces of silver to make these purchases, the Chinese money-changer, thinking he was dealing with simple Tartar Lamas, allowed a high rate, and gave full weight, but endeavoured to cheat in the calculation; the missionaries, however, with their arithmetic, were too much for the Chinese money-changer, with his saopan, and got their full change. Their means compelled them to put up with second-hand sheep-skin cloaks, and fox-skin caps; they took, however, the precaution to treat them with a mercurial process to get rid of the vermin, a necessary operation before they could venture to wear them.

At Koko-Khoton there are five great Lamaserais, in each of which there are more than 2000 Lamas, besides fifteen smaller ones; 20,000 is thus a low estimate for the number of Lamas in this famous city. The chief of the whole is a " Hobilgan," established at the Five Towers; that is, a Lama, who, having by abstraction and study, obtained Boodhism, has been transmitted since by regeneration. In the reign of Kanghi, the *Geesoo-Tamba resided at Koko-Khoton; and that emperor paid him a visit when on an expedition against the Ooloo, or Ili tribes. The insolent Boodh received him without rising or taking the least notice, whereupon a military mandarin, in attendance, drew his sword and slew him on the spot. The city was immediately in *émeute*, and the Emperor's person was for some time in great danger: most of those with him were sacrificed, and amongst them the perpetrator of the violence on the Geesoo Tamba. The Khalkhas tribe of Mongolia took up the cause, and declaring that the

---

* M. Timkowski says " Koutouktou, in Mongol, and Goussée (Geesoo) in Tibetan, is the name of the highest class of the priests of Boudha; the one resident at Ourga is called by the Mongols, Gheghen Koutoukton "

Geesoo Tamba had re-appeared in their country,
established a grand Lama with that title at Grand
Kouren. Everything was ripe for an insurrection;
but Kang-hi proved equal to the occasion. He
immediately courted the Delai Lama, of Lassa,
and through him gained over all the Lamas of
Tibet and Tartary not already compromised in the
quarrel. Thus he restored tranquillity without
further collision or violence. The Lamas of Grand
Kouren, however, wear to this day a black border
on the collar of their yellow dress, in memory and
in mourning for this slaughtered Geesoo Tamba.
It was settled on this occasion that the Geesoo
Tamba should remain at Grand Kouren, and an
Hobilgan replace him at Koko-Khoton, and that
the regeneration of the Geesoo Tamba should
always take place hereafter in Tibet, by which
means the local influence and attachments of this
hierarch are much diminished. Koko-Khoton is
an university in which Lamas from all parts come
to study and take degrees, returning afterwards to
their provincial establishments. Lamas are of
three kinds—the religious, who devote themselves
to study and abstraction, and become teachers,
and eventually saints; the domestic, who live in
families, or attach themselves to tribes and localities; and the itinerant, who are always moving
from convent to convent, and travelling for travel's

sake, often without aim, not knowing at all where
they are going. There is no country that some of
these have not visited, and when they have a religious or partisan feeling they must be the best
spies in the world.

In the monasteries of Mongolia there is a strict
religious discipline, but each Lama has generally
his cows and sheep, as well as a horse. Almost
every establishment is nobly endowed, and the
funds are distributed on fixed days in the year in
proportions, regulated by the rank attained by
each member. But each Lama is free to seek
other emoluments, such as by practising as a phy-
sician, or by performing domestic religious services, or by casting horoscopes, or in any similar
manner, not inconsistent with the profession of a
Lama. Some attain wealth, which, having no
families, they generally spend prodigally. The
number of Lamas in Tartary is extreme; almost
all the younger sons are devoted from infancy to
this destiny; the eldest only being brought up as
laymen, to tend the flocks and keep up the family.
The younger brothers have no choice, but have
their heads shaven from childhood. It is said to
be the policy of the court of Pekin to encourage
this multiplication of Lamas among the Tartars,
in the idea that it checks the increase of popula-
lation. The shaven are, however, the most intel-

ligent and influential, if not the most numerous
body of these sons of the desert, and the Chinese
pay court to them assiduously in consequence.
In China Proper the corresponding class of Bonzes
is quite neglected by the government, and has
sunk intothe most abject poverty. The reason is
obvious. A regenerated Boodh of Tibet or Tartary
can at any time call round him thousands of devoted Lama followers, ready to sacrifice their lives
at his bidding; and these no less than the lay
Tartars, whom they lead by their religious influence, have a high military spirit, and the recollection of the past glories of their race in the days
of Jungeez and of Tymoor, to excite them to great
enterprises. It is hence the study of the Chinese,
and a recognised part of their policy, to associate
this influence with the State, just as the Church
in Europe is made by most governments an engine
of order and of civil government. To effect this,
the government of Pekin contributes largely to all
the monastic institutions of Mongolia, Tibet and
Tartary, and supports the hierarchy and even the
theocracies established by aspiring priests in
various parts, as at Lassa, and at the Grand Kooren
of Oorga, using these institutions to control the no-
bility as well as to leadthe mob. But there is at each
seat of theocratic government a skilful Chinese di-
plomatist,who advises, and even controls,the deified

Lama; and who, upon occasions for political action of any kind, is the prompter and director of all affairs, holding the strings and wires that move the puppet, while they treat him with all outward respect and reverence.

On the fourth day of the ninth moon the missionaries left Koko Khoton, but found the utmost difficulty in leading their camels through the narrow, ever-muddy streets. The country they now passed through was rich and highly cultivated. On the second day they put up at an inn, where they met a singular character, who called himself a " Tartar-devourer," and who was an agent to recover debts owing to Chinese. The next day they arrived at Chagan-Kooren, or the " White Enclosure." As they reached it, they fell in with a caravan of camels laden with merchandize of the west, which extended for fifteen lis, or five miles. It had been travelling for five months across the desert, and came probably from Kashghar.

They arrived at the town late at night, and found a lodging with difficulty at a hospitable Mongol's. They were now approaching the Hoang-Ho, or Yellow River, and learned here that the inundations were out, and the passage across nearly impossible. They determined, nevertheless, to attempt it. Chagan-Kooren is a new town, built with great regularity, having broad sheets

and open squares; but the inundation reached to
its suburbs, and the camels after leaving it had to
proceed on muddy embankments, through fields
with the water up to their knees; while the whole
plain before them had the appearance of a great
lake. At a village which they reached, after a
laborious but short march, they bargained with
some boatmen for the passage, and were asked
two thousand sapeks to carry them over the first
channel. They reduced the charge to eight hundred, and were so conveyed to a station on the
bank of the main stream, which was rapid but not
very broad. Here they bargained again to be
carried across this channel for another thousand
sapeks, making an ounce of silver for the whole
passage. Their camels were taken into the boat at
the second passage, an enterprise effected with extreme difficulty. They had forded the first stream
under bad guidance and were nearly lost. The
missionaries, after crossing this main stream, had
yet a third branch, the Paga-Gol, to get over, and
a march across muddy inundated fields to make
before they could reach its bank. That march
effected, they remained some days on the northern
bank of the Paga-gool, disputing about the terms
of transport. At last they effected the transit by
the favour of a fisherman, who having been bitten
by a fierce dog, came to them for medical treat-

ment. When the styptic they administered had
been applied with success, the fisherman, being
ashamed of his inability to pay the usual fee, undertook for the passage of the party on reasonable
terms. The right of ferry, it may be observed, is
a monopoly enjoyed under a royal grant by a
family, whose exorbitant demand was beyond the
travellers' means, and this was the cause of their
long detention at this point.

Beyond the Paga Gol lies the country of the
Ortoos, which extends a hundred leagues from
east to west, and sixty-six from north to south.
In A.D. 1635, the tribes of this region sided with
the Manchoos, in their contest with the last of the
Ming dynasty, and thus came into great favour
with Kanghi, who declared them the most honest
and intelligent of his subjects, and the best cattle
breeders of all the Mongol Tartars. But the
country is a sandy desert throughout, producing
nothing except wild hemp, the dried remains of
which formed a fuel much superior to the argols,
or camel's dung, which our travellers usually depended upon for their meal. But the great want of
this country is water, and owing to the sterility in
consequence, the Ortoos are in the greatest misery,
and beggars are here more numerous than in Ire-
land. In crossing the Ortoos territory, the travellers encountered a storm of wind, and rain and

snow, that reduced them to the greatest possible
state of distress and difficulty. But they found by
good fortune, some caves and deserted rock habi-
tations, which gave them shelter, and afforded the
means of drying their clothes and refitting the
caravan. They met here a Tartar, who told them
that the caves had been thus prepared by a party
of Chinese who had settled there to cultivate the
adjacent lands. When they grew rich and insolent,
the Tartars resolved to expel them, and accordingly
drove cattle into their ripe fields, destroying the
entire crop, which had led to the Chinese decamp-
ing in a body about two years before. After
leaving these caves, the missionaries experienced
the extreme cold of one of those winds of Tartary,
which are described as so terrible. The cold was
too severe to allow of their continuing the march,
and it gave them full employment to collect fuel
for a good fire. After a halt of two days, the wind
becoming more moderate, they resumed their
march, but could not draw their tent pins without
first heating them several times with hot water
poured round them. They had, however, no sooner
commenced the march than they felt the heat
quite oppressive; such are the alternations of tem-
perature in that terrible climate. On the 15th
day of the Ninth Moon, the missionaries fell in
with pilgrims on their way to Rashchooren, to see

a Lama, who had vowed there to cut open his
bowels in public. For this the devotee prepares
by long penance, prayer, and abstraction: on the
day appointed he sits on an altar, and deliberately
ripping open his belly, lays the bowels before him,
and so falling into a kind of trance, answers
oracularly all questions put by the pilgrims. The
operation finished, he gathers his bowels up again,
and reciting a long prayer, readjusts his girdle as if
nothing had happened. We commend this miracle
to the Magician of the North. The missionaries
resolved to go a little out of their road to witness
the exhibition, but lost their way, and passed a
miserable night in the desert. Beyond the monastery of Rash-chooren, they came to the salt
lakes of Dabsoon-noor, which, though nearly dry,
required great care in the crossing, owing to the
multitude of quicksands, and general treachery of
the soil. Round these lakes are rich pastures for
cattle, and especially for camels. Two days' journey
beyond them, the travellers halted, still amid rich
pastures, and purchased a sheep for a feast from a
Lama, who procured them also an accomplished
butcher, and brought his family to partake of the
dainty meal. The description of these festivities
will well repay the reader; but we refrain from
entering into the details. On the next day, after
a long march, the water had to be drawn from a

deep well, the mouth of which was closed with a large stone. Another long march brought them to the "Hundred Wells;" and on the day after, they met the Prince or King of Alishan, on his way to Pekin to render homage. Three Tartars of this prince's suite passed the night with the missionaries, and explained the relations which subsisted between Alishan, and the court of Pekin. The tributes paid by all these Tartar chiefs are little more than nominal—a camel, or a horse of particular breed, or any special rarity the country may produce of the vegetable or animal kingdom, forms the tribute. One of the chiefs of the Chakar tribes, for instance, pays tribute in pheasants' eggs, which are used to give lustre to the hair of the imperial concubines. But all such tributes must be offered in person by the head of the principality, and the visit is required to be annual, unless in consequence of the distance the period is extended to three years as a great favour. Arrived at Pekin, the tributaries are treated very unceremoniously; they have no separate audiences, but on great days, like that of the New Year, or the Emperor's birthday, they stand round and see the Imperial countenance approach from a distance. Immediately on his appearance they must all fall on their knees, and perform the Koton, never rising till the Emperor has passed. On the other hand, all these petty chiefs are pensioned, some receiving as much as £2000 per annum, and others less. The stipends are paid in hard silver, at the time of presenting the tribute, but occasionally the tributaries receive plated ingots instead of genuine ones.

The information given by these Tartars of the character of the Alishan country, and of its recent sufferings from drought, decided the missionaries to take a more eastern route through Chinese territory to the Koko-noor valley, crossing again the Hoang-ho, or Yellow river, for the purpose. By this route, they would pass within two days' march of the native country of their servant, Sambda Chamba, which was to him a source of great satisfaction, as he had not seen his family for eighteen years. From due west, the travellers now turned a little to the south, and were directed on their march by a Tartar, whose information confirmed their map: but the water at their next stage was very putrid, and required to be purified by charcoal. They passed here through mountains of schist, which had the appearance of having been heretofore washed by an ocean wave, and presented the most grotesque forms, besides being covered with shells and marine fossils, and being worn into caves evidently by water action.

After crossing this range, the Yellow River was seen at its foot, still a magnificent stream, and was passed to the little town of Shé Tsui Dze at a reasonable ferry charge. The missionaries now found themselves upon Chinese ground, at the end of two months from the date of their departure from the " Valley of Black Waters." At Shé Tsui Dze, they put up at the hotel of " Justice and Compassion." From the day of their leaving Koko Khoton, they had not seen the interior of a habited house. They were here in comparative comfort, and their host was a communicative person, from whom they obtained much intelligence as to their future route. After two days' rest, the travellers proceeded, and crossed the Great Wall, which surmounted the rising ground beyond the river. It was here a barrier of little strength and rough workmanship. Works of irrigation, and other evidences of Chinese skill and enterprise, were apparent on their line of march; and the contrast of the province of Kan-sou with the arid desert of the Ortoos was remarkable. The first halt in Kan-sou was at Wang-ho-po, where they fell in with a Chinese caravan, bound like themselves to Ning-Hia. On the road to this last city, they found guardhouses at every half league, consisting of square towers, built for the protection of travellers. Arrived at Ning-Hia, a demand was made for passports by three pretended public officers. In the night, their camels made free with some fresh

oziers on a cart within reach of their long necks.
A tumult arose in consequence, which ended in a
demand upon the missionaries to make good the
damage. But a jury of bystanders, a tribunal
always available in China, adjudged the reparation
to be made by the hotel-keeper, as he had been
forewarned. Resistance to anything unjust or
unreasonable is always the best course even for
strangers.

Ning Hia is a city of the first rank, but it be-
trayed unmistakeable signs of decadence. A magnificent road carried them to Hia-ho-po, at the
hotel of which, named "the Hotel of Five Feli-
cities," a white-buttoned official impudently required them to make way for his master, a mandarin of high rank, with a large suite. But here also
the travellers stood on their right, as being the first
arrived, and thus shared fairly the accommodation.
Two more days carried them to Chong-Wei, a fortified town on the banks of the Yellow River, which
contrasted favourably with the misery of Ning-Hia;
but to their wonder, the river was here without
boats. At Chong-Wei, the Great Wall was again
passed, and the travellers found themselves again
amid the sandy mountains of Alishan, showing no
signs anywhere of vegetation, and moving with
every breath of wind. It is from these sands that
the Yellow River acquires the tint whence it de-
rives its name. The camels sank in the loose sand

to their knees at every step, and the travellers were
compelled to dismount, in order to pursue their
laborious journey.   These sands seem to be blown
up by the western winds of the great Shamo desert,
and are piled up in hills on the bank of the river,
but are there arrested.   An oasis in the middle of
these sands, called Chang Lieon-Choui (Ever
Flowing Waters), was their resting-place, a delight-
ful spot, where their only complaint was of over-
charge for their night's accommodation.   From
this village, they followed for some distance the
high road to Ili, the penal settlement of China in
the extreme north-west. The stations on this road
are maintained by convicts, whose banishment to
Ili is remitted on the condition of their providing
water and provisions to public travellers, who else
would find none.   Along this road they proceeded
till they again crossed the Great Wall, and soon
after an interior barrier, called that of San yen
Tsin, at the resting-place beyond which they were
again importuned for passports, as a plea of extor-
tion, but again successfully resisted.   They were
now in the province of Kan-Sou, a well cultivated
wheat and pasture country ; but they encountered
here a dry tornado of a most formidable character,
which, if it had fallèn upon them while amid the
sands of Alishan, must infallibly have destroyed
the whole party. After a day's rest at a respectable
farm, they reached Choang Long, or Ping-Fang,

the hotel of which was kept by a Chinese, who at once asked them if they were not Ing-kilee (English). This they denied, and a bystander relieved them from the embarrassing question by saying, " Don't you know that those English have all blue eyes and red hair." " True," said the master of the hotel, " I did not think of that ; besides those Ing-kilee never leave the sea, and can't ride, but shake like little fish out of water when they mount on horseback." At this hotel they met a grand Lama, who was a regenerated Boodh of the Khalkas tribe, returning from Tibet. All but our travellers prostrated themselves before him. The saints' curiosity brought him, however, to terms of familiarity with them, notwithstanding this want of respect, and he asked if they were Russians or English (Peling)* from the Ganges and Calcutta. He had travelled between Tibet and the country of the Khalkas more than once, and had there heard of these two nations, but knew nothing of France.

The next stage, after leaving Choang-Long, was Ho Kea-y, which also has another name, Tai-tong-Fou, which is less used. Here they put up at the hotel of " Temperate Climates," where they rested for eight days for the sake of their cattle, whose

* Peling is the Tibetan corruption of the word Feringi, itself a corruption of Frank, the Oriental word for European.

backs were chafed by the long travel. Being near
the country of their Chiaour servant, Sambda
Chamba, they gave him leave to visit his family,
which he found in much distress, and relieved at
the expense of his own wardrobe. Leaving Ho-
Kiao-y, they crossed a high range called Ping-Kiou,
the summit of which they reached only at mid-day,
beginning the ascent at sunrise. It snowed as they
passed; but in the descent on the other side, they
felt inconvenienced from the heat. The pathway
was so steep, as to compel the travellers to dismount; and one of their camels twice rolled over,
but without suffering much injury. There is coal
in this range of hills: much of it was met under
conveyance to the river on bullocks, mules, and
other animals. On the further side of the Ping-
Kiou range they came to a village of stocking-
knitters, called Lao-Ya-Pou, five days' journey
beyond which is the city of Sining-Fou, situated
in a well cultivated country, abounding in tobacco;
but the road of the last day was amid rocks, and
along the line of a torrent presenting many dangers. The route of the missionaries Grueber and
Dorville fell in here with that of our travellers, but
they had come across China Proper by Singanfoo.
At Sining, strangers are not received into the
hotels; but there are separate lodging-houses,
called Sie-Kia, where they are boarded as well

as lodged for nothing, the keepers of the houses
drawing their profit from the agency of purchases
and sales for these strangers, which is proportion-
ately extortionate. The missionaries having contributed nothing in this way, paid for their accommodation. The route after this was rocky, and
crossed several torrents, and the Great Wall was
passed twice before they reached Tong-Keon-ool,
a small but thriving commercial town, in the valley
of the Koko-Noor, full of inhabitants of all races,
from all quarters, and speaking all languages. The
missionaries were here also received at a free
lodging-house, kept by a Mussulman. It was now
the month of January, and consultation was held
upon their further proceedings. To pass the mountains into Tibet at this season was full of hardships,
and dangerous in many respects. Yet they could
not think of abandoning the object of their long
journey, and in summer, the torrents and melting
snows would present even greater difficulties. After
a stay of six days, while they were yet deliberating,
a party of Khalkhas Tartars arrived on their way
from Grand Kooren (Oorga) to Lassa, to do homage to a new Geesoo Tamba, declared to be regenerated in a family of that country. There were
but eight men of the party, but each had more
than one horse, besides forty camels for the baggage of the whole.

The missionaries rejoiced at first in the opportunity of continuing their journey in such company, but upon enquiring they gave up the idea,
finding that these Tartars travelled fifty or sixty
miles a-day, which, with their own small supply of
cattle, was impossible, and they had not the money
to purchase more. These Tartars were all nobles
of the royal race, and were visited by the young
prince of the Koko-Noor Valley, who advised the
missionaries to wait for the return, in spring, of
the Tibetan mission, then at Pekin, which advice
they determined to follow. At eleven leagues
distance from Tang-Kiou-ool, in the Sifan pasture
district, and not far from the lake of Koko-Noor,
is the famous monastery of Koon-boom, containing near four thousand Lamas of all nations.
Thither M. Gabet went to seek a Lama preceptor
to teach them Tibetan, while they waited for the
caravan of the mission then at Pekin. He found
and engaged a cousin of their servant Sambda
Chamba, a Chiaour Lama, named Sandara, thirty-
two years of age, who had lived for ten years in a
Lamaserai of Lassa, and who understood most of
the languages of China. He was extremely intelligent, and had passed through strange adventures, having at one time been an actor in a
travelling Chinese company; but he was cunning,
and not the best tempered of preceptors : how-

ever, he was most useful in the menage, and
arranged for their removal to the Koon-boom
monastery at the beginning of the Chinese year,
after about a month's residence at Tang-Kiou-ool.
At Koon-boom they obtained lodgings from a
generous priest, whose liberality had ruined him,
and who could take no rent consistently with the
rules of his order. Opposite to them, in the same
court, lived a niggardly Chinese Lama, of great
reputed wealth. On one side was a medical prac-
titioner, who stuttered to a degree almost destroying his respiration when he attempted to speak, a
defect which the Chinese Lama's apprentice took
mischievous delight in mimicking. These neigh-
bours and their host they met daily, but very
seldom visited or received each other in their
apartments. The Lamaserai of Koon-boom, with
its 4,000 Lamas, covers the two sides of a mountain ravine, and consists of a number of white
mansions built upon either side, with Boodhist
temples interspersed. At every step you meet
Lamas with yellow mitre-shaped caps, and red
cloaks, walking gravely, as though absorbed in
thought. At the time of the arrival of the missionaries, they were preparing for the feast of
flowers, which was expected this year to be held
with unusual magnificence. On the 15th of the
first month of the year this festival recurs; but in

lieu of flowers, there are figures of all kinds prepared of frozen butter, which twenty chosen Lamas
work upon for weeks before, wetting their hands
in cold water to prevent the butter from being
melted as they model it.   Strangers from all
quarters flock to the festival, and the missionaries
were most agreeably surprised by the exhibition.
The accuracy with which the features and dress of
all types of the human race were represented in
bas relief, especially the skin-dress of many, ex-
ceeded anything they had yet seen in art, and all
this was in butter, destroyed and cast into the
ravine, to become food for crows, the day after the
festival.   While examining these displays of art,
the Grand Lama of Koon-boom came with much
ceremony and state to see the festival; he was a
very ordinary-looking person of forty years of
age, but his costume struck them as corresponding exactly with that of their own bishops, even
to the violet chape.

The Koon-boom monastery is situated in the
Amdo district, south of Koko-Noor, and is surrounded by barren red and yellow mountains.
It is the birth-place of Tsong-Kaba, of whose
miraculous conception and infancy strange legends
are current.   He was born A.D. 1357, and devoting
himself when quite young to a life of privation
and abstract study, became, according to these

legends, the pupil of a stranger of the west, described as of great learning, and of peculiar
physiognomy, being remarkable for the length of
his nose. This stranger, after teaching all his
learning to Tsong-Kaba, laid himself down on
the top of a mountain and slept the sleep of
death, never to awake, being very probably frozen
to death. Upon this Tsong-Kaba resolved to travel,
and went first south into Yunan, whence he made
his way after a time to Lassa. There a super-
natural injunction bade him fix his residence.
He accordingly preached his new doctrine there,
and introduced new prayers and forms of ritual,
and gained many converts. His sect were dis-
tinguished by yellow capes,—red being the former
colour. Gaining ultimately the ascendant, Tsong-
Kaba founded the Kaldan monastery, nine miles
from Lassa, in A.D. 1409, being then fifty-two
years old. This monastery still exists, and numbers more than 8,000 Lamas. In 1419, the reforming saint quitted this world for the celestial.
Tsong-Kaba, besides reforming the ritual, revised
and published a new version of the doctrinal
scriptures of Sakhya-Mooni; the great founder of
the religion, under the name of the " graduated
road of perfection." The missionaries saw reason,
in the conformity of ritual, as well as of costume,
especially in this sect of Lamas, for believing that

the preceptor of Tsong-Kaba must have been a
stray member of the Romish Church, who found
his way into these regions a century after Rubruquis and Marco Polo. His doctrine and ritual are
now the prevailing forms of worship in all Tibet,
Mongolia and Tartary, and have been adopted in
many Chinese monasteries. That of Koon-boom
was built some time after his decease at his birth-
place, and there is a miraculous tree shown, which
is said to have grown on the spot where his hair
was shorn on his becoming a Lama, on every leaf
of which tree there is a letter of the Tibetan
alphabet distinctly marked. The missionaries saw
the tree. It was old, with a stem that three men
could scarcely circle in the girth, but was not
more than eight feet high; the Tibetan letters
were well formed, and seemed engrained in the
leaf as it grew. They testify to the miracle, but
could not at all account for it. We presume the
letters to be written upon the young leaves with
some substance that affects their growth and
texture, and so remains indelible. The tree, they
say, is of a species that no one has seen else-
where. The Emperor Kang-hi, when he made a
pilgrimage to Koon-boom, covered the tree with
a silver dome, and gave an endowment for the
perpetual support of three hundred and fifty
Lamas, which the monastery still enjoys. The

missionaries speak highly of its discipline and management, and testify to its well-merited celebrity as an university for the instruction of Lamas. There are four great classes, with separate professors for each. First and highest, the faculty of mystical doctrines, and of the life of contemplation which leads to sanctification; Second, the faculty of the liturgy, including the study of all religious ceremonies; Third, the faculty of medicine, including botany and pharmacy; Fourth, the faculty of prayer, which is obligatory on all, and consequently is the best filled. There are thirteen classes in this branch of study only, the books of prayer being most numerous, and very voluminous, and the students being graduated according to their progress in these books. No one is advanced for age or length of study; very young persons, even boys, take often the very highest places in the hierarchy. The place is given after strict examination, but a handsome present to the institution, or to the examiners, mitigates much of its severity. The lectures are given at all seasons in the open air, and the lessons having been recited, one of the pupils is called upon generally to maintain a thesis upon any subject. He must answer all opponents, and if victorious, is carried round the school-yard on the shoulders of the vanquished. The whole disputation is conducted in

E

the Tibetan language, no other being taught or
admitted in the schools. Discipline and attention
is strictly enforced by censors, who carry iron rods
with which they punish summarily any delin-
quents. The proctors and their bull-dogs are dis-
tinguished by a grey dress and black mitre. They
have great power in the streets of the town, as
well as in the courts of the monastery, and there
are Lama judges for more serious offences. For
any petty theft, the culprit is marked on the fore-
head and cheek by a hot iron, and expelled.

Our two missionaries, with the aid of their preceptor " Sandara," prepared a Tibetan abstract of
the Scriptures, and a summary of the principal
doctrines of their own faith. The report of their
employment spread in the monastery, and excited
many anxious enquiries; so much so, that they
began to hope for extensive success in winning
converts to their faith; but their preceptor was
a confirmed sceptic. The stuttering student of
medicine was much better disposed, though full
of superstitions. He proposed to them one day,
to assist in a charitable ceremony for the benefit
of lost and forlorn travellers. It consisted of the
very simple process of stamping the figure of a
horse, caparisoned, on little pieces of light paper,
and giving them to the strong winds on a mountain top, with certain prayers. The young student

had the most perfect faith that many a poor wanderer would be relieved by this charitable sending of horses in all quarters.

The missionaries had resided three months at Koon-boom, when they received a civil message that the time had expired when they could live as stranger guests, dressing and comporting themselves as they pleased. If they remained longer, they must wear the mitre and costume of the monastery, and matriculate. They objected on the score of religious scruples, and were accordingly advised to remove to a less strict monastery at Chogortan, especially devoted to medical students. This advice they readily followed, and had no reason to repent the change of their residence. Before taking leave of Koon-boom, M. Huc devotes a chapter to the precepts of Boodh, and to the introduction of this religion into China. What he cites, and the facts he mentions, are curious and highly interesting; but through the late Mr. Ksoma de Koros, and Mr. Turnour of Ceylon, we have much more full details on the subject of this religion, derived directly from Tibetan and Pali sources.

The Chinese give the year, B.C. 1029, as the date of the birth of Sakhya-Muni, or Boodh, and the year, B.C. 951, for that of his death; but they admit that the religion was not introduced into China until 1,000 years later. They state the book of the Forty-two Precepts, from which the missionaries give extracts, to have been translated into the language of China, in the year A.D. 68. A comparison of many epochs has established in India the date, B.C. 628, for the year of the birth of Boodh; and B.C. 543, for that of his decease. We ask not for him greater antiquity than this, but shall reserve the examination of this question, and especially the discussion of the claim of the Boodhist sacred books to greater antiquity than our own, until we have carried our missionaries to their journey's end.

The climate in the elevated region of the Koko-noor, wherein the missionaries made this long sojourn, is so severe, that snow falls nearly throughout the year, though the latitude is only 36° north. In July, however, there is a sudden change, and vegetation proceeds as if the earth were in a state of fermentation. The mountains are suddenly covered with verdure, and flowers show their bright colours on all sides. At this season the camels of our travellers lost their long hair, and were for some days quite uncomfortable, but it grew fast again, and the coat thus shed proved a valuable acquisition, being converted into cords for fastening the loads. Chogortan is the Richmond, or the Brighton, to which the Lamas of

Koonboom resort for recreation in summer; and here especially came, at this season, the whole faculty of medicine, to collect simples for their pharmacy. In the plains round about were rich pastures, from which the monastery was supplied with argols for winter fuel. The missionaries have a special dissertation in this place, upon the merit of the argol of different animals; that of goats and sheep stands in the first class; camels in the second; kine of all kinds in the third; horses, and animals of that genus, in the last, because the dung of these animals burns too quick, and gives a disagreeable smoke.

The Chogortan Valley, in consequence of its favoured pasture-grounds, is subject to the attacks of brigands, not plundering as individuals, but in organized bodies and tribes. The Lamas of Koonboom take to arms immediately on hearing of the approach of these banditti, but not with any effective organization, so that the valley is sometimes swept before any succour can arrive; and the missionaries were witness to the confusion resulting from an incursion of this kind during their stay.

It was the end of September, 1845, before the Tibetan mission made its appearance in the valley of the Koko-noor, on its return to Lassa from Pekin. Immediately, on hearing of its approach,

our travellers made their preparations so as to be
ready to accompany the caravan. The supplies
they laid in were, three bricks of tea, two sheep's
stomachs of butter, two sacks of flour, and eight
sacks of Tsamba, that is, of roasted barley meal,
to be mixed with the tea, which is the universal
food of Tibetans, without being satisfied with
which, there is no passing by this route into
Tibet. The above supplies were for the two missionaries, with two servants, four camels, two
horses and a mule, a condition of baggage and
commissariat for such an expedition, that would
satisfy even Sir Charles Napier. A good supply
of garlick, a specific recommended by the people
of the country to prevent ill consequences from
bad atmosphere and nauseous vapours, was the
only further article provided. For the conveyance
of these extra supplies a horse and camel were
added to the original establishment with which
the missionaries had reached Koonboom, and a
young Lama was hired as helpmate to Sambda
Chamba, in tending the cattle.

With this preparation, the missionaries made a
march of four days to meet the Tibetan mission
on the banks of the Koko-noor lake, or rather
inland sea. They passed on their way to the lake
the Lameserai of Tansan, having about 200 Lamas,
and found magnificent pastures on the plains

near the lake. These travellers are the first Europeans from whom we have any trustworthy notice of this lake from personal examination. They describe it as about one hundred leagues in circumference, and as salt as the ocean. They state it also to be subject to some kind of tide, but this we think must be a mistake. Towards the south end of the lake there is a rocky island where a few Lamas have established a temple with some huts for residences. There is no communication with them except in winter over the ice, for on the whole lake there is not a single boat. The Lamas, however, are liberally supplied in that season by the shepherds. There are twenty-nine banners of subject princes who divide the pasture-plains of Koko-noor amongst them, paying tribute to China. The plundering tribes are Eastern Tibetans, of the Sifan race, who live in the Bayen Kharat mountains, near the sources of the Yellow River. They are called Kolo, and are Boodhists, but have added to their mythology a special God of plunder.

The missionaries remained near a month on the banks of the Koko-noor, waiting for the Tibetan envoy's caravan from Pekin. It arrived towards the end of October. It used to be the custom for the Tibetan mission to travel yearly to Pekin, but in 1840 the caravan was attacked by the Kolo

robbers, whom they beat off, but found next day
that the Chanak-Kampo, or Lama ambassador, had
disappeared in the night attack, whether slain or
not, was never thoroughly ascertained. Again, in
1841, a second officer of the same rank received
a severe wound, of which he died shortly after. In
consequence of these casualties, the Emperor made
the mission triennial, instead of annual, and it
was the return of that of 1844 that formed the
present caravan. It consisted, by our traveller's
estimate, of 15,000 yaks, 1,200 horses, and as
many camels, and about 2,000 human beings of
whom all the mounted were well armed. The
Chanak-Kampo rode in a litter carried by two
mules; the caravan had an escort of 300 Chinese
soldiers, from the province of Kansou, and 200
mounted Tartars, who were to conduct it to the frontier of Tibet, but no further. The caravan generally
started three hours before sunrise, so as to come
to the new ground by noon, and so afford the cattle
grazing time; two guns gave the signal for preparation and departure, and the march was a general
move without much order. After a journey of six
days, the Pouhain-Gol, a river that falls into the
Koko-noor, had to be crossed; it ran in twelve
channels, not very deep, but the frozen edges made
the passage difficult and disagreeable.

Our travellers made acquaintance, in this

journey, with three Lamas, who had travelled over
the whole of Mongolia, to collect subscriptions for
the erection of a grand temple near Lassa. They
had been eminently successful, and were bringing
back means sufficient for their grand design; but
at Koon-boom were overtaken by an order from
Pekin, and the principal emissary was sent on to
Lassa for trial, on the charge of fraud and forgery,
and his treasure was placed at the disposal of the
Dala Lama to abide the result. Five days' march
beyond the Poohain-gol, the caravan came to
a small river, on the other side of which was a
deserted Lamaserai, which had been beseiged and
ravaged by the terrible Kolo plunderers. Here
the Chinese escort left them. On the 15th November, they entered the Tsaidam district, occupied by Mongols, and crossed the river of that
name. The soil is dry and rocky, and produces
borax, which is collected in pits, where it crys-
tallizes freely. On the further side of this valley
was the dreaded Boorhan-boota Mountain. On
the eastern and northern side of this range the air
is so impregnated with carbonic-acid gas, that
unless there is a wind to sweep it off, animals can
scarcely pass without suffocation. It is like the
valley of the Upas, in Java, which is fatal from a
similar cause. Our travellers passing at a time of
calm, experienced severely the effects of the cor-

rupted atmosphere. But this difficulty was trivial
in comparison with the passage of the Chuga
mountains some days after. The ascent from the
north-east was easy, but the summit was no
sooner reached than a wind met them in the face,
in the midst of deep snow, that made the descent
dangerous in the highest degree. They could not
venture to face this wind, and sat with their faces
to the horses tails. Monsieur Gabet reached the
bottom with his nose and ears frozen, and suffered
so severely in other respects, that his recovery was
at one time despaired of. At the halting-place
they had to scrape away the snow in search of
argol fuel, to make a miserable fire, the heat of
which was insufficient to boil their tea.

The miseries of a Tibetan journey had now fairly
commenced; all the travellers marched in mourn-
ful silence amid snows that proved every day fatal
to many of the cattle, and the road was strewed
with the bones of men as well as of animals, to
remind them of the perils by which they were surrounded. Monsieur Gabet fell sick, to a degree
that made him quite helpless, in consequence of
his sufferings in the passage of the Chuga; yet
there were still two months of journey before them
to Lassa, and no possibility of halt, no comforts,
no medicines. In the beginning of December,
they reached the famous Bayen Kharat chain of

mountains, which stretches, from south-east to
north-west, between the Hoang-Ho and Kin-Cha-
Kiang rivers. They were now close to the sources
of the former, which lay two day's journey to
the East, but could not be visited. Here they held
council how best to effect the passage of the dividing
range. It lay before them, covered with deep fresh
snow. The day was calm, but much of it had passed
when they reached the foot of the ridge. On the
other hand, there was a probability of a wind arising
by the morrow, which would be fatal in the then
condition of the snow. The caravan was divided in
opinion; but our travellers were of the party for
proceeding, and they scrambled over the fresh snow
without accident. Luckily, the next day also was
fine, and those who had stopped came over likewise,
without any one being lost in an avalanche or a
snow-wreath, which was looked upon as extreme
good fortune. They rested on the side of a frozen
lake, depending on the argols of previous caravans
for fuel; and moved, next day, to the bank of the
Mouroui-Oossoo, the name here given to the river
called below the Kin-Cha-Kiang, and in the plains
of China, the mighty Yang-Tse-Kiang, or Blue
River. They passed it over ice, and witnessed a
strange spectacle in the passage. A string of more
than fifty wild yaks had been frozen up at the very
moment of swimming across, and remained there
fixed in death, their eyes having been pecked out

by crows and eagles. Wild yaks and wild asses
are common in the most elevated regions of Tibet,
and are seen wandering in herds, seeking fresh
pastures.

The caravan here separated, the camels preceding, because capable of making longer marches,
and of moving more rapidly than the loaded
yaks. By a gradual further ascent, our travellers now reached, at last, the dividing land between the waters of China and Tibet, the highest
elevated region, perhaps, in the whole world. It
was mid-winter, and for fifteen days the wind blew
over the plain with murderous severity. During the
whole of this time the cold was so intense, that
though they wore flannel shirts, and over that a
coat of fox-skin, and over that a lamb-skin jacket
or spencer, and a large cloak of sheep-skin over all,
and carried their Tsamba paste for refreshment on
the day's journey next to their skin, yet they never
took it out to eat during the march in this elevated
region, without finding it frozen. It is wonderful
that the human frame should endure this conse-
cutively for days together. The cattle required to
be enveloped in felt wrappers, but were nevertheless decimated in the terrible march. And here
we must be permitted to complain of our travellers
for starting on such a journey without even a compass, a barometer, or a thermometer. A solar
microscope it seems they had with them, but a

compass to give the bearings of remarkable peaks, and a thermometer to show the degree of cold, and the boiling point of water, would have given scientific results of the highest possible interest and value. Lieutenant Strachey, the officer of the Indian government, who wintered at Ladâq, and penetrated in the spring and summer of 1848, to the sources of the Shayek, and to the Pangong Salt Lake, in order to determine the boundary of the Chinese territory towards the Indus, crossed several passes of 18,000 and 19,000 feet of well ascertained height; and we expect shortly from the brother of this officer some curious scientific particulars, the result of a careful survey and examination of a considerable area of territory at the sources of the Sutlej. These French missionaries give us no means of comparing observations made at the sources of the great rivers of China, with those of these western explorers, and we may wait long for another journey into the regions crossed by the perilous route we are here tracing.

More than forty men of the caravan were left on the road frozen during the fifteen days of painful march over this table-land, and no one could stop to relieve, or even to bury, those overtaken by the frost. M. Gabet's illness and sufferings increased to such a degree at this period of the journey, that he could neither ride nor walk; he was consequently sewed up in his cloaks and blankets, and so carried, like a bale of goods, on a camel. But he recovered when the extreme cold was somewhat mitigated, and the cutting wind had ceased. In the midst of this march, the travellers fell in with a party of Kolo brigands, who, however, showed great respect for the Lamas of the west, and declared that they had no wish to plunder what the caravan was carrying back to the Delai Lama; but would never suffer the wealth of Tibet to be carried to Pekin, in order to be laid at the feet of a Chinese emperor. Soon after this rencontre, the caravan approached the Tant-La* pass, the summit of which they reached, after six days of continual further ascent. At the top was another table-land, along which they travelled for twelve days; but the wind had ceased to blow, and the sun was now radiant and reviving, and M. Gabet recovered wonderfully under its influence. After thus crossing this high dividing ridge of Tartary, the descent was from mountain to mountain, in steps each day of reduced elevation. In the valleys, hot springs were very frequent. After some days of rough travel, the missionaries reached a plain of good pasture, where

* Throughout Tibet, as far west as Ladaq, a mountainous pass is called La. This is the first on the road from Pekin to Lassa, that bears this name. It is an evidence of the commencement of the use of the Tibetan language as the vernacular.

they gave their worn-out cattle a halt of two days, during which shepherds brought them fresh meat, a luxury they purchased with such articles of Pekin manufacture as they could spare; but just as they were on the point of sitting down to a luxurious meal of roasted mutton, so procured, the cry of fire! fire! arose, and they found that some injudicious members of the caravan had ignited the grass to windward, and the flames were coming down fast upon their encampment. The tents were saved with extreme difficulty, but the long-haired camels would not move out of the way of the flames, and one of them was so dreadfully burnt as to be rendered quite unserviceable. Following down a valley, the travellers came now to the first Tibetan village, called Na-Pchu, or Khara-ossoo, both meaning, one in Tibetan, and the other in Mongolian, Black Waters. The village is inhabited by Tartar shepherds. The missionaries sold here their three serviceable camels for fifteen ounces of silver, and gave the poor burnt one into the bargain. With this money they purchased six yaks, to convey their baggage to Lassa, and the assistant camel-driver, who had proved a great rogue, was discharged. The thieves of Napchu are described as expert and most audacious.

There were yet fifteen days of march from this

village to Lassa. Our missionaries travelled the
remainder of their journey in company with some
Mongols of Kharchin, who along with a regenerated Boodh were on pilgrimage to the holy city.
The Chaberon, so these sainted hierarchs are called,
was a young man of eighteen, and was proceeding
to graduate and study in one of the Lamaserais of
Lassa. A prince and several nobles of Kharchin
accompanied him, and he was watched, rather
than attended, by two aids-de-camps, who permitted him no recreation, but compelled him always
to sit in state, and act and talk the regenerated
Boodh—a miserable state of existence! He was,
however, allowed to visit and converse with our
Lamas of the West, and is described as an intelligent well-disposed youth, who enjoyed much the
privilege of holding rational converse.

The route between Na-Pchu and Lassa, is described as rocky, fatiguing and difficult, and sometimes even highly dangerous, but the caravan was
approaching civilization, and everything seemed
now to smile. The passage of the Koiran range of
mountains presented most difficulty. On the fifteenth day from Na-Pchu, they reached Pampoo,
called on maps Panctou, a valley interspersed with
farm-houses, on the banks of a considerable river.
Here they had again to change their carriage
cattle, and provide asses in place of their yaks.

The cold had sadly disfigured their bearded coun-
tenances; but they did their best, with their limited
wardrobe and means, to make a respectable appearance on their arrival at Lassa. Asses having
been provided, after some delay, in sufficient abundance for the whole party, the missionaries, with
their Mongol associates, scaled the high mountain
range, which still lay between them and Lassa,
called the Boodha-La, and so reached the city at
last on the 29th January, 1846, eighteen months
after their start from the Valley of Black Waters in
Mongolia.

The houses of Lassa are described as large,
and are fresh whitewashed and painted every year,
so as to present a gay appearance, but within they
are filthy in the extreme, cleanliness being no characteristic of a Tibetan or Tartar. They found a
lodging at Lassa, in a house of entertainment,
where there were fifty other lodgers, and hired an
upper room, to which they were compelled to
mount by a ladder of twenty-six steps. It had
for chimney a hole in the roof—not a comfort-
able substitute in the depth of winter; but even
this was preferable to retaining the smoke of the
argol fuel in the room they inhabited, which those
below were compelled to submit to. The city of
Lassa has no wall, but is surrounded by garden
suburbs. The streets are broad, well laid out,
and clean enough, but the suburbs are filthy in

the extreme. There is one quarter, however, the
houses of which are described as most picturesque,
the walls being built of the horns of cattle and
sheep, intermixed with infinity of designs, and
cemented together with mortar between. We cite
this description of Lassa, because the city has
never, that we know, been yet described by any
European traveller. Mr. Manning, who went there
from Calcutta, in 1811, intending to penetrate
into China by that route, was seized and sent back,
and saw very little of the place; and his Chinese
companion, being handed over to Chinese courts
of justice, was never afterwards heard of. Mr.
Manning went then by sea to Canton, and died
there, without giving to the world any result of
his travels and researches.

The French missionaries were assured by Tibetans that Mr. Moorcroft had also been at Lassa,
and a Kashmerian merchant introduced to them
a Moosulman named Nishân, who declared himself to have been Mr. Moorcroft's servant, and to
have accompanied him in tours of exploration
made in different directions, in quality of a Mahommedan cattle merchant, speaking Persian. We
know that Moorcroft died of fever caught in
Koondooz; this person must, therefore, have been
one of his companions, who assumed his name.
The traveller, whoever he was, is said to have been

murdered by robbers in the Gnari province, near the sources of the Indus. No intelligence corresponding with these particulars has ever reached any British officer; and on the other hand, there has been much exploration lately in the direction of Gnari, and the Chinese frontier in that quarter has been laid down by Lieutenant Strachey, before alluded to; so that such an event, if it were really true, could scarcely have escaped them. We must admit, however, that the motives for concealment were of the strongest on the part of the Chinese frontier officers.

The palace of the Delai Lama at Lassa, called the Lassa Morou, is built on an isolated rocky hill, at a short distance to the north of the city. It is of stone, and of large dimensions, with a high gilt dome, exhibiting, say our travellers, much architectural beauty. We presume the style and character of the edifice not to be very different from those described, and of which we have drawings, in Turner's Embassy to Tibet. Round the palace are a multitude of Lamas' edifices of all sizes. The Delai Lama is the Pope of Tibet; but as he is supposed to be always in the state of abstract meditation for the benefit of mankind, his temporal authority is exercised through a deputy, called the Nom-Khan, who is also a sanctified Lama, enjoying the relative posi-

tion towards the hierarch of a Romish cardinal.
About two hundred years ago, the women of
Tibet, being much given to dress and libertinage,
corrupted the Lamas to a degree to bring their
holy order into bad repute. The then Nom-Khan
accordingly issued an edict, that the women should
never appear in public without first smearing their
faces with a black disfiguring paste. Strange to
say, this order was obeyed, and the practise is
still observed, but without much benefit to morals.
Father Grueber notices this habit of smearing the
face to have prevailed in his time, which was one
hundred and eighty years before the visit of our
travellers. The women are described as active,
industrious, and managing persons, like those of
France, and not at all likely to be content with
the place assigned to women in the social system
of India and of Western Asia, nor do they submit to seraglio discipline.

The position of the Chinese at Lassa is peculiar.
In the time of Kanghi, the influence of the name
and authority of the Delai Lama was of such importance in his relations with Mongolia, that this
emperor established envoys to pay court to the theo-
crat, and exalt his pretensions to supreme Papal
authority. These envoys were called Kin-chai, and
there were two in Tibet. When the Nipalese in-
vaded that country and plundered Teeshoo-Loom-

boo, recourse was had to China for military aid, and the Chinese army, after defeating that of Nipal at Tingri, compelled the court of Katmandhoo to sue for peace, and send a mission of tribute to Pekin every third year, as we have before related. Consequently, upon this, the Chinese Kinchais at Lassa came to exercise as much authority there as a British resident does at the court of a protected state in India. In the thirty-fifth year of Kien-Long (A.D. 1770), which was before this war with Nipal, and before the mission of Captain Turner, the two envoys (Kinchais) at Lassa, seized and beheaded a Nom-Khan during a visit of ceremony. An *emeute* was the consequence, which ended in the massacre of every Chinese in Tibet. A long war, and the invasion of Tibet by a Chinese army followed. The result was to re-establish the Chinese Kinchais at Lassa, with equal, if not superior, influence to that they before enjoyed, and this was confirmed and much augmented by the events of the war with Nipal. But there are very few Chinese troops in Tibet to support the influence and authority the Kinchais exercise. There is, indeed, a line of guard-houses all the way between Lassa and Yunan, for the purpose of keeping up the communication, and another line of guard-houses, with small garrisons, is established along the Bootan and British frontiers.

At Lassa, however, the head-quarters of all these posts, there are only a few hundred troops. These receive their pay from China, and are relieved every third year.

The principal Chinese envoy at the time of the arrival of our missionaries was, as we before said, the well-known Ki-Shen, the great councillor of state, who had been sent to negociate with the British admiral and with Captain Elliot at the commencement of the war with China in 1840. The result of his negotiations was, it will be recollected, a treaty or convention, containing a stipulation for the cession in full sovereignty to the British Queen of the island of Hong Kong. This was a *sine qua non* of Lord Palmerston's instructions, and was agreed to most unwillingly by Ki-Shen. When the treaty was sent to Pekin for ratification, this article was looked upon there as disgraceful, and the negotiator was recalled and sentenced to confiscation, and to exile to Ili; his great credit at court and known talents alone saved his head. The issue of the war which followed having proved his superior wisdom, and the affairs of Tibet requiring a man of vigour and ability, Ki-Shen was partially restored to rank, and appointed to the mission there. The case forms a curious passage in that country's history.

The Nom-Khan of Lassa is himself a " Chaberon," or regenerated Boodh, selected for the office of civil administrator by the Delai Lama. The Nom-Khan whom Ki-Shen found there had been nominated long before, and in his time three successive Delai Lamas had died very soon after reaching the age of majority. This occasioned great scandal, and it was openly said that all three events were the work of the Nom-Khan. The first Delai Lama had died of strangulation, the second was killed by the fall of the roof of his bed-chamber, and the third was poisoned at a meal, along with several of his familiars. Add to this, the chief Lama of the Kaldan monastery, close to Lassa, had died suddenly in the same way.

The Nom-Khan was a Sifan noble of Yang-Tou-See, consequently a subject of China. He was rich, and by his liberality had obtained a large following, the Lamas of the Sera monastery especially being much devoted to him. There are under the Nom-Khan four state officers, called Kalons. These combining, made a secret representation to the court of Pekin of the crimes and cruelties of the Nom-Khan; and it was in consequence of their representation that Ki-Shen was ordered from Ili to investigate and redress these evils, and was vested with extraordinary powers for the purpose. Upon his arrival in

Tibet, he paid court to the Bundshan-Rembou-
chi,* the great Lama of Teshoo Loomboo, and to
the four Kalons or ministers of the Nom-Khan
at Lassa. With their help he obtained evidence
to prove the charges of murder against the Nom-
Khan, who was accordingly brought to trial, and
on being confronted with the witnesses, confessed
his crimes, and signed the record which contained
the evidence of his guilt, together with his accomplices' confessions. It was countersigned by
all the high officers of Tibet, including the Teeshoo
Lama, and the case was so sent to Pekin for adjudication. Three months afterwards, the imperial mandate arrived, sentencing the Nom-Khan
to exile on the banks of the Sagalien in Manchoo
Tartary. The sentence was immediately placarded
at Lassa, and the Nom-Khan was placed in con-
finement. The Lamas of the Sera monastery,
however, to the number of 15,000, rose in insurrection, and gaining the ascendancy at Lassa, re-
leased the Nom-Khan, and wished to carry him
back to his palace in triumph. But he refused,
saying he must make the journey to Pekin, in
order to explain the case, and enlighten the em-

* Turner calls this officer the Punjin-Rembochay. M. Huc
says he claims equality with the Delai Lama. The place we
call Teeshoo Lomboo, after Captain Turner, M. Huc calls
Jachi Loomboo, and translates, " Mountain of oracles."

peror, for submission was his duty. The Lamas of Sera were disconcerted by this refusal, and returned at night to their convent. In the meantime, Ki-Shen, who had escaped the first violence of the insurgents, concerted measures with the Kalons, and brought next morning an armed force into the plain between the monastery and Lassa, and so reduced the rebellious Lamas to submission. The Nom-Khan was dispatched a few days after in a palanquin, by the route of Se Chouen, to the place of his exile. The accomplices, however, were left to the Kalon magistrates of Lassa, and were not severely dealt with.

The selection of a new Nom-Khan fell on the Chabron, or regenerated Boodh-Lama of Ranchan, a youth of only eighteen years of age. The first Kalon was accordingly named regent, and it was with him and Ki-Shen that the missionaries had to deal in January and February 1846. What passed is curious, and deserves full mention.

The missionaries reported themselves to the authorities at Lassa, as Lamas of the west come to enquire after, and to preach the truth. They were immediately visited by an inquisitive Chinese who came to enquire what they had to sell. "Nothing," they said, "but their old saddles." "Exactly what I want," said he; and in bargaining, asked multitudinous questions calculated to

F

elicit all particulars regarding the strange visitors to the holy city.

Four similar visits of inquiry for merchandize did the missionaries receive on the same day. It was evident that these were all spies. At the dinner hour they were summoned to the presence of the Kalon, regent, along with their servant, Sambda-Chamba. On arriving at the palace, this functionary surveyed them curiously for some time without saying a word, whereupon they said to one another in French : " He seems of good dis- position, we shall fare well." Though said in a whisper, they were immediately called upon to repeat what they had said ; which they did aloud in French. An appeal was then made to all pre- sent, to know if any one understood the language. The answer being in the negative, they were called upon themselves to translate, which they did faithfully into Tibetan. The regent was pleased with the compliment, and made a long speech to explain how it was his duty to be well disposed. He then asked whence they came; they said " From the West." " From Calcutta ?" he asked; they replied, " No; from France." " You are assuredly Pelings?" (English) said the regent. " No ; we are French." " Can you write ? " said he. They said " Yes ; " whereupon ink and paper were provided, and they were told to write something in their own language. They wrote

"Que sert a l'homme de conquerir le monde entier, s'il vient a perdre son ame." They were made to write the translation of this in Tibetan, Mongolian and Chinese, which they did, exciting the admiration of the court at their learning and profound doctrine. In the midst of this, Ki-Shen came to the palace, and the examination was renewed before him in a different spirit. They saluted him in the French form, without falling on their knees, merely taking off their caps and bowing low. "'Tis well," he said, "you follow the customs of your country; they tell me you speak correctly the language of Pekin. Let us converse in that." The missionaries said their language would be found faulty by such a judge, but his intelligence would penetrate the meaning. "Pure Pekin!" he exclaimed, "you French must have great facility in the acquisition of languages." "Yes, we are French." "I knew some Frenchmen in old days in Pekin," he said. "You might also have seen some at Canton," they replied; but the recollection was not agreeable to their questioner, and he frowned. "You are Christians," he said. "Yes." "I knew it! and you are here to propagate and spread your religious opinions." "It is our only object." "What countries have you passed through?" They named China, Mongolia and Tibet. "Who did you live with in China?" They refused to answer this

question, even though threatened; but told freely
where they had learned the languages they knew.
" And who are you?" he said, turning sharply
to Sambda-Chamba.   " A native of Ki-tou see."
"Where is that?"   " In the district of San-Chouen,
in the Kansou province." "Ah! subject of the central nation! down on your knees, before your Emperor's representative.   On your knees!" he repeated, and was instantly obeyed. "As a subject of
China, I am your judge; say, where you met these
foreigners?" Sambda-Chamba replied frankly, not
denying that he was himself a convert to the Christian faith; which he could not believe to be proscribed, because it enjoined him only to do good,
and to shun evil. " True," said the Commissioner,
" but what induced you to enter the service of
these foreigners?" He denied that he knew them
to be foreigners, or otherwise than as good men.
" What wages do they give?"   He said, " None,
but his board and lodging; he was with them for
the sake of his soul, regarding them as his spiritual
teachers."   " Are you married?"   " No! I was
a Lama, before joining them." The next question
drew a blush from Sambda-Chamba; he did not
answer it. And the missionaries protested against
such imputations, declaring the thought or mention of such things to be equally against their religion and their morals.   At this Ki-Shen felt re-
proved, and broke up the examination, saying it

was late, and he should require to see them again
next day. From this examination they were carried again to the regent, who promised his support,
gave them supper, and questioned them several
times over on the subject of maps, and notes of
their route. They told him candidly that they
had a printed map of China with them, by which
they had been guided on their journey. The
regent heard this with some anxiety, fearing it
would give them trouble; the great dread of the
Chinese being, exploration by Europeans to ascertain the geography and resources of their country.
Rooms were prepared for the missionaries this
night in the palace, where they were now, in fact,
prisoners. They were carefully waited upon, and
found good beds provided; they passed the night,
however, in great anxiety as to their future fate,
and found a resource and comfort in prayer. Early
the next morning they were visited by the chief
Kashmerian merchant, who came to condole with
them, and to tell them to prepare next day for a
close examination of their baggage. This was the
work of the Chinese Kinchai, he said, against the
wishes of the regent, but they must submit. All
these precautions, he further told them, were the
consequences of Moorcroft's explorations; amongst
whose effects, after he was murdered in Gnari, the
Chinese had found many maps and notes illustra-

tive of the geography and resources of the entire
country.

Early next morning, the Tibetan regent made
the first examination of their baggage with all
forms, prior to sealing it up. A crucifix was the
first thing that engaged his attention, and he
laughed heartily when the missionaries said it was
with that that they had come to make the conquest
of Tibet. A careful list was made of everything
to the most minute article, and the whole baggage
was then carried under seal to the court-house,
where Ki-Shen was waiting. "Have you only these
two trunks of baggage," he asked. "Nothing
else," said they; "you may open them and see
what they contain." "Are they mine," said he,
"that I should open them, and expose myself to
your reproaches, if anything should be found wanting? open them yourselves." Everything was then
laid out, and examined with the utmost curiosity
by all present. Amongst the articles were some
books and lithographic drawings, which excited
much admiration. Ke-Shin took upon himself to
explain the great progress the French had made
in the arts, and he asked if the missionaries had no
watches, telescopes, or magic lanterns. They
pointed to a solar microscope, the only instrument
of that kind which they had with them, and put it
together, nobody but Ki-Shen himself having the

slightest idea of its use. He asked them to exhibit it; but they put it up again immediately, saying, "We are here under examination and trial, not to make exhibitions." He then asked for the maps, which were produced, being one of the world, on Mercator's projection, and another of China, both printed in France.

The regent gave them a look which seemed to say, "You are ruined, and have signed your death warrants;" but the missionaries appealed to Ki-Shen's intelligence and knowledge of things to distinguish printed from manuscript maps, and to satisfy himself that these were not of their own drawing. He at once recognised them as printed maps, and pointed out the distinguishing marks to the regent, who seemed much relieved, though he could not understand the difference.

At the request of both these officers, the missionaries pointed out on the map of the world, the site of all the different countries. Calcutta was a first object of enquiry, and when it was indicated, they remarked how near it was to Lassa. "Never mind," the regent added, "the Himalaya lies between us and the English." Kishen was quite familiar with every article used in the ritual of the Catholic church, having been governor of the Picheli province when the Christians were persecuted and expelled. These, therefore, created in him no suspicion, and the examination ended in a decision that the missionaries were plain men, without deceit, and should be left at liberty. The regent was delighted at this issue of the examination, and the head of the Kashmeer merchants provided a banquet to greet them on their return home; and further purchased, on the regent's account, their two white horses for two ingots of silver, each of ten ounces, a liberal price, exceeding their value in the then condition of the cattle. One of the ingots they gave to Sambda Chamba, as a compliment on his discharge, which was to him a fortune, not unmerited by his services.

The next day, the missionaries became the regent's guests, and improved their acquaintance with him to terms of familiarity. At the house he assigned to them, they prepared an oratory with a crucifix, and other attributes of religion, and commenced their religious functions in a manner to excite curiosity, and to give them the hope of making converts. They began thus to flatter themselves with the promise of great success in their mission, and amongst others, reckoned even upon the probability of making some impression on the regent himself. He was a man of great experience of the world, as well as of high literary reputation in Tibet, and he delighted in discussing doctrinal questions with the missionaries, acknowledging fully the paramount necessity of enquiry, for the purpose of ascertaining where truth lay, for the

good of the soul in perpetuity. He acknowledged
the truths and moral precepts of Christianity,
claiming for pure Boodhism perfect correspondence
on these points, and alleging the errors pointed
out by the missionaries to have been the result of
erroneous teachings of ignorant or half-informed
Lamas. The two points of disagreement were
the creation of the world, the Mosaic account of
which the regent could not accept, and the doctrine of transmigration, which was to the missionaries equally irrational. In discussing these differences, the regent was more than a match for
the missionaries, while they conversed in Tibetan,
and they were compelled to call in the Cashmerian
chief merchant to interpret the arguments they
wished to enforce. The regent seeing this, and
promising to renew the discussion when they were
more familiar with the language, gave them his
nephew for preceptor, to perfect them in Tibetan;
and in the meantime, confined himself ordinarily
to conversing about Europe, its arts and habits,
concerning which he showed great curiosity, especially after having witnessed with great wonder an
exhibition of the solar microscope. He mastered
completely the Roman alphabet, from a copy of it
made for him by the missionaries, and was particularly interested in descriptions of steamboats,
railroads, balloons, and daguerreotypes.

With Ki-Shen also the missionaries had very
friendly relations. He questioned them frequently
about England and Queen Victoria. His idea of
Prince Albert was singular; he conceived that,
because the British constitution gave him not the
kingly power, he must be to the queen, what queens
of China are to emperors and other royal person-
ages of the east, and no more. He asked after
Lord Palmerston and Captain Elliot, and was not
surprised to hear that the latter had been recalled
at the same time that he was himself disgraced.
" He was a good man but irresolute," said Kishen;
" was he put to death or exiled?" "Neither one
nor the other; these things are not managed so
summarily in Europe." "I know," said he, "your
mandarins fare better than we do. Our emperor
cannot know everything; yet it is he only who
judges, and none dare speak in his presence. If
he says, this is white, we say, truly so, it is white;
if soon after, he points to the same thing, and says
it is black, we fall on our faces and say, yes, it is
black. But if one, more bold, ventures to suggest
that the same thing cannot well be both black and
white, the emperor will say, 'That is true;' but
the offerer of such a suggestion will probably lose
his head. Ah! we have no assembly of chiefs as
you have, to control the actions of our emperor."

Ki-Shen told them freely how the affair with the

English had been treated in 1839-40. The Emperor called his eight Choung-Tangs to council, and stated the case. He said, "These western mariners are very rebellious and refractory; they must be chastised as an example to all others." Having thus stated his own opinion, he asked the advice of his council. The four Manchoo councillors fell on their faces, and said, "Yes, yes, 'tis the sovereign's wish and order." The Chinese Choung-Tangs then prostrated themselves, and said, "Yes, yes! 'Tis the heavenly will of the Emperor;" and so the thing was settled. Kishen himself acknowledged his conviction that the Chinese would never be able to contend with Europeans till they adopted their weapons and discipline; but added, that no one dared to advise the Emperor to this effect, or he would lose his head.

The missionaries had the means, through their intimacy with the Tibetan regent, of informing themselves fully of the doctrines and customs, as well as of the constitutional forms of the Tibetan theocracy. The Boodhist religion has no eternity of punishment. Everything proceeds from God, and will return to him; but the soul passes, in transmigration, to inferior or superior animals, according to its desert. There are six grades of animals vested with souls. Angels, demons, men, quadrupeds, birds and reptiles. A soul in each state has its means of attaining greater perfection; the highest of all is to be absorbed into the Divinity, whence again living Boodhs are detached, to take a human shape, in order to recal men from errors and teach the road to perfection.

The highest of existing regenerate Boodhs are the Delai Lama of Lassa; the Band-shan Remboochi, of Teeshoo Loomboo, the same who was visited by Captain Turner, in the time of Warren Hastings; the Geesoo Tamba of Grand Kooren, at Oorga, on the borders of Siberia; and the Changkia-fo, or great almoner of the court of Pekin. Of all these the Delai Lama of Lassa is the pope, or spiritual guide of all Boodhists. He was only nine years old when our missionaries were there, and had been then recognised pope for six years, having been taken from an obscure family of Sifans, in the province of Ming-chen-tou-tse. When this Boodhist pope dies, everybody falls to meditation and prayer to discover the new birth. Prayer barrels*turn with redoubled vigour. All who

---

* Every Lama has his prayer-barrel. Prayer and meditation being regarded as the only effectual means of attaining sanctification, the continued repetition of the mystical " *om mani padme hom,*" is considered as the first essential of faith. Hence the number of repetitions is the test of merit; and for multiplication of them the devise of turning a barrel, on which the words are written. has been imagined, and obtains universal credence in its efficacy.

fancy they have a regenerate Boodh in their families give notice, and a council of holy ones, that is, of Kotooktoos, sits, and selects three infants, who are sent for to Lassa to be examined. For six days they are shut up, and the examiners devote themselves, this while, to earnest meditation and prayer. On the seventh day they write the names of the three infants on golden plates, and place them in an urn. The senior Kotooktoo draws the lot; and the child whose name is drawn is immediately proclaimed Delai Lama, and carried in state through the town; while the two rejected children are returned to their families, with liberal pensions. Our missionaries wished to be presented to the Delai Lama, and the regent had arranged for their presentation, but an alarm was raised that the foreigners might communicate the small-pox, for it so happened, that this disease broke out soon after the arrival of the caravan with which they had travelled to Lassa; thus they lost the opportunity of witnessing the forms and ceremonies of this extraordinary court.

While they were thus living at Lassa, the guests of the regent, and honoured and respected by the entire population, a storm was brewing in a quarter they little suspected. They meditated opening a communication, through Calcutta, with the China mission, of which they had heard nothing since they undertook this journey; and M. Gabet pro-

posed to attempt the route, through Bootan for the
purpose, when the Chinese commissioner, Ki-Shen,
sent for them one day, without warning, and after
much prelude of compliment told them he was
quite sure the climate of Tibet was too cold, and
the country unsuited for Frenchmen accustomed
to the life they had led; that they had better,
therefore, prepare for their return. The missionaries asked if this was his advice or his order? He
said, coldly, " Both." They objected, saying, as a
matter of advice, they were not disposed to adopt
the suggestion, being quite prepared for all the
difficulties and inconveniences of a residence in
Tibet; on the other hand, being under the protection of the established governor of the country,
they did not recognise his right to order them out
of it. " You, strangers, and foreigners! do you
claim the right to remain?" said he. They replied,
boldly, that they conceived they had the same
right as was conceded to the natives of India, of
Kashmeer, and of Mongolia; while his title of
Kin-chai, or resident-ambassador, showed himself
also to be a stranger. " I, a stranger!" said
Ki-Shen, starting up, " I, who hold the Imperial
commission, by right of which I have tried and
sentenced the Nomkhan of this country." " But
he was a native of China, and a guilty man," said
they; " we are men of God, preaching only the

salvation of souls." " I know," said he, "you are
good men, and zealous in your calling, but your
religion has been condemned by the Emperor."
They declared that they needed not the Imperial
sanction to perform their religious duties. And
with this the conversation for that day closed.

They had now indeed braved the lion in his den.
They went forthwith from the Kin-chai to the
regent, in order to claim his protection. He was
well disposed to grant it, if left to himself. But
the Kinchai declared that he was specially com-
missioned to protect the interests of the Delai
Lama and of the Boodhist religion, in Tibet,
and that he could not permit so great a danger as
the continued residence in the country of men
who preached doctrines subversive of both. Their
aim, he said, was to subvert Boodhism, and establish
their own faith. If they succeeded, what would
become of the institutions of Tibet, and of the
Delai Lama, and what would the Emperor say to
him for allowing it? The Tibetans, he declared,
knew not the extent of the danger, and seeing the
men to be virtuous, and of good life, and of great
comparative learning, believed them innocent on
that account, as well as good; but their virtues
and their learning only made them more dangerous in his eyes, for the Tibetans would be unable
to cope with them on points of doctrine, and many

simple people would be won over from the faith of
their ancestors, if the mischief were not prevented
in time.

The matter was argued for several days between
the regent and the Kin-chai, and protocols were
exchanged in due form. The Tibetan regent submitted in the end; the missionaries themselves so
advising, for peace-sake. They went accordingly
to Kishen, to announce their readiness to obey his
mandate, and proposed to leave the country by the
route of India. He said he had already prepared
everything for their departure; that they should
travel with an escort as far as the frontier of China,
but could not be permitted, as they desired, to go
by Bootan to Calcutta. They exclaimed against
the cruelty of compelling them to make again a
perilous journey, such as they had just gone
through, and hinted that their country's government might well take umbrage at such treatment
of its innocent subjects. Ki-Shen coolly replied
that what the French government might say or do
was nothing to him, he knew his duty to his own
government, and should deserve, and be punished
with, death, if he suffered their stay in Tibet, and
did not send them back to China.

Next day, Ki-Shen again sent for them, to read
the report he had prepared of their case. He said,
he wished to report fairly as well as correctly, and

therefore had sent for them to hear what he had written, in order that anything erroneous might be corrected. M. Huc, after hearing the draft read, said he had one thing to represent, but must do it in secret, as it was of more importance to Ki-Shen than to themselves. He at first insisted on what M. Huc had to say being publicly stated, but on his still refusing, Ki-Shen cleared the room, when M. Huc told him he had entered China by Macao, in the second month of the twentieth year of the reign of the Emperor Tao-Kwang, when Ki-Shen was himself viceroy at Canton, and it would be for him to say whether this circumstance should be reported or no. " Does any one know this?" said the Kin-chai. " Nobody." He then tore up the report, and wrote another, with his own hand, saying nothing of the time of the missionaries entering into China, and praising highly their learning and general character.

This matter being so settled, it was arranged that the missionaries should start after the festival of the new year of Tibet, which is one month later than that of China, and is kept like our Christmas and New Year, with nightly wakes, and revels, and festivities. On the third day of the moon the Lamas are let loose from all the adjoining monasteries, and for six days after that, the city and neighbourhood is inundated with them, and the greatest confusion and disorder prevails.

There are, near Lassa, three great Lamaserais;
those of Kaldan, Preboung, and Sera, each of
these having 15,000 Lamas attached to it. They
are distant twelve, six, and two miles respectively
from the town. The Lamas of all three deem it a
point of duty to make the pilgrimage to the holy
" Morou" convent, at Lassa, in order to receive
there the benediction of the Delai Lama, for the
new year; and the feuds and jealousies of these
institutions produce, consequently, innumerable
quarrels at this season.

The missionaries were, during these saturnalia,
preparing for their journey back to China. They
took affectionate leave of the regent, and of the
Kashmerian head merchant, with both of whom
they had established the most friendly relations.
Through the latter, they now made the attempt
to send a letter to France by Calcutta, but we are
not informed whether it was successful. They
parted, likewise, with the faithful Sambda-Chamba,
and so prepared to wait on Ki-Shen, in order to be
forwarded as he might direct.

The mandarin-commandant of their escort, was
named " Lee," the " Pacificator of Kingdoms."
He had commanded on the Goorkha frontier of
Nipal, and wore a blue button. Though only
forty-five years old, he seemed upwards of seventy,
being completely worn out by service, as well as

debilitated by a life of excess, and by indulgence
in spirituous liquors. He had the rank of Tou-tse,
and was entitled, therefore, to an escort of fifteen
men, now that he was retiring from the service
and returning to China. He was a man of much
intelligence, but, like most Chinese, a perfect free-
thinker in matters of religion.

To this man the missionaries were first introduced on the day of their departure; and they
went with him to Ki-Shen, who now announced that
they were to return by a different route from that
by which they had come; but, he trusted, neither
so long, nor so difficult ; that he could not provide
them with palanquins; so that they must ride with
the escort, and would find relays of horses, called
oollas, at the different stages and guard-houses,
for which he gave the order. He told them they
would be conveyed at the public expense to Si-
Chouen, where the Governor, Pao, would provide
for them. He next made a speech to the " Pacificator of Kingdoms," advising him to give up
drinking ardent spirits; and then he paid him on
the spot 500 ounces of silver, as retiring bounty
for his services. Lastly, he made a speech to the
escort, enjoining them to do their duty; and when
these ceremonies had been gone through, he took
the two missionaries apart, and told them he himself should soon be recalled to China, and he

wished two large boxes of treasure to be carried thither in advance.* These he asked them to take amongst their baggage, and deliver safely as directed, at Ching-ton Fou, the capital of Se-chouen. Then publicly warning them against thieves, he bade them farewell.

The Kashmerian chief merchant rode with them to the Boo-Choo river, where they found a Tibetan escort of seven men and a Deba, appointed by the regent to accompany them. The river was crossed in a skin boat by the missionaries and the Pacificator, the cattle and baggage having crossed in canoes.

The missionaries were now travelling by relays of the ordinary Chinese post, on the direct line to the central provinces of China. After crossing the river on their first march on the 15th March 1846, they went for some time along a highly-cultivated valley, the fields marked by stone-wall enclosures, to Detsin, a large village six leagues or eighteen miles from Lassa. Here they were received in state by the village authorities, headed by the Deba Lama, who commanded the escort of Tibetans assigned by the regent for their protection. He proved a very intelligent and most useful intermediary for communications with

* Ki-Shen was shortly after appointed Governor of Se-chouen.

the people of the country. His name was Sham-
Chand. They supped here with the Pacificator,
who lent them his itinerary, which they studied
and copied. From Detsin the route still lay in
the same fertile valley, gradually ascending towards a mountain range. After twenty-five miles
(eight leagues—eighty lis) of this march, they
stopped at a convent in ruins, situated at the
extreme verge of cultivation; but they had still
twelve miles to ride to the post station of "Mich-
hou-Koung," which they reached only after dark.
They were compelled to halt the next day, for
want of the relay of horses called the "Oola."
There would be no travelling in these hill countries, if the obligation to furnish men and cattle
were not imperative on the population that in-
habits them. This duty is enforced more strictly
than the payment of taxes, and is indeed almost
the only state requisition made on the population.
Every village and every family acknowledges the
liability, and must either serve in person or provide a substitute, or furnish cattle. The Chinese
officers abuse this regulation, and use influence to
get an order for a larger oola than they require,
that they may take an equivalent for the excess.
The Pacificator of Kingdoms had procured our
missionaries to be set down as requiring twelve
yaks for their luggage, although they had but

their beds and two portmanteaus. Like all of his nation, he was exceedingly avaricious.

The oola being at last provided, the caravan started next morning from Mich-hou Koung, and for five days had to pass through ravines and rocky mountains, along the line of the same river that they had crossed on leaving Lassa. The description given of this part of the route is very ungeographical, the direction by compass even not being stated. It is, indeed, not quite clear whether the route lay down the course of the Sampou, or Bramapootra, or up one of its tributaries; but we presume the latter, because, after five days' travel, they ascended the Looma-Ri mountain, or rather table-land. It was not steep, and the ascent was made without dismounting; but the table-land extends for forty lis, or about thirteen miles, and the descent to the station of Ghiamda on the other side was difficult, from the quantity of ice and snow. After leaving the table-land, they had first a dense forest to pass in a close ravine, and then to scale a mountain-ridge on foot, from the top of which the descent was made by a slide over congealed snow. There were at Ghiamda two mandarins and eighteen soldiers, who received the Pacificator with a salute, and the Tibetan civil authorities paid a similar compliment to the missionaries and their Deba. At Ghiamda they stayed two days, partly detained

by rain and tempestuous weather, but mainly be
cause the oola was incomplete. At Ghiamda, also,
the local Deba made the missionaries a present of
hair spectacles, to guard their eyes against the glare
of snow, a necessary precaution, for from this point
they had for many days together nothing else but
snow to cross. A little way out of Ghiamda, a torrent
was passed on a bridge of firs; and for three days
afterwards, there were no villages, nothing but
Chinese guard-houses for the relays, with a few
shepherds huts; still the horses and cattle of the
oola were always ready. On the fourth day, after
crossing on ice a large lake, they came to the village of Adza, where the Chinese itinerary says
unicorns are to be found, that is, the Cherou
antelopes, described by Mr. Hodgson.

From Adza to La-Ri is only fifteen miles, but
between lies a range of mountains covered with
perpetual snow, and for five days it had been
falling fresh, making the passage very dangerous.
It was determined, after some consultation, to
proceed, if the weather continued fine, next day,
sending the yaks in advance to beat down a pathway. The sun shone bright, and the ascent was
successfully made of this mountain of spirits.
On the other side, near the top, was a glacier
which was passed by all the party on the slide, the
yaks leading, fortunately, without loss or injury.

Passing downwards, thence, along the river, the caravan soon arrived at La-Ri, which is reckoned to be one hundred-and-one leagues, or about three hundred-and-three miles from Lassa, and was thus reached on the fifteenth day. There is a provision depôt at La-Ri, under a Leang-Tai, or Chinese civil officer, who made the excuse of ill-health for not visiting them, but the Pacificator said it was avarice that prevented the compliment being paid, in order to save the presents that would be required. On the first march from La-Ri, they crossed a lake about three miles long by two-and-a-half broad, quite frozen over, and lodged for the night at a village called Tsa-chou-ka, close to some hot springs. Next day they crossed the Chor-kou-la, equalling in elevation and difficulty of passage the La-Ri. After the ascent, the journey lay for several days over a table-land of broken ridges, with terrible precipices sometimes on both sides, and with so little footing, as to be quite unsafe, otherwise than mounted on the trained cattle of the country, and these often were lost by a slip or false step. The road, indeed, was occasionally formed of wooden pathways let into the mountain side without, of course, any railing.

After two days' journey of this kind, the caravan reached Alan-To, where they were congratulated by the Deba on their good fortune in having lost no lives among the precipices of the approach.

From Alan-To, a march of ninety lis, or about 27 miles, brought them to Lang-ki-choung, a picturesque village in a wooded valley, called by the Chinese, on account of its fertility, Kin-Keou, " Golden Dell." Here the Pacificator was disconcerted by the announcement that the oola was ready, but that the Tanda pass in advance was closed. Our missionaries looked into the itinerary they had borrowed, and found it stated in truth that the Tanda pass was the most difficult of the entire journey. People were sent to examine the route, and reported it quite impracticable. They were in consequence detained for some days at Lang-Ki-Choung, and found amusement in playing chess with their fellow-travellers, the game being well known even in this wild region. All this while the yaks of the place added to those of the caravan were employed in beating down a passage through the snow of the pass. On the fourth day the passage was declared to be sufficiently practicable, and they started. The ascent was so steep and slippery that the only method of mastering it was to hold on by the tails of their horses, and both would often have slidden over into the valley they had quitted, but for the walls of snow left on either side. M. Gabet was quite exhausted by this

G

ascent, and must have been left behind, if the
Tibetan escort had not taken him among them,
and with great efforts pushed him up to the top
of the pass, scarcely sensible. On the summit of
the mountain was a body of Lama pilgrims, on
their return from the Lassa-Morou, all lying down
to recover their breath, which they had quite lost
in the painful ascent. The descent on the other
side of the pass was even more precipitous than
the ascent, and an ass was lost over the precipice;
but, with this exception, all reached Tanda in
safety. From this station to Lha-dze, a distance
of one hundred and ten lis, or thirty-six miles, the
route proceeds along the plain or valley of Pian-
pa, for half the distance, and then down the bed
of a torrent to what river tributary we seek in
vain; we guess it must be one of the streams that
flow into Assam, and not into the Irawadi, or any
river of Siam, or into the great river that flows
through Cambodia, the main stream of which was
yet far to the east. Klaproth would carry into that
stream the rivers of Lassa, which we know now to
form the Brahmapootra river, debouching with the
Ganges into the Bay of Bengal. The rivers of
Burma and of Siam reach not to so high a latitude.

From Lha-dze to Barilang is one hundred lis
or somewhat more than thirty miles, crossing
the famous mountain Chak-la, one of the passes

which the Chinese call " Life-claimers." It was found fatiguing, but was passed without accident. From Barilang, after a march of equal length in a valley studded with herdsmens' huts, and herds of wild yaks, they reached Chobando, a considerable town, with its houses and Lamaserais painted red. Here is a military station of twenty soldiers under a Tsien-Chong, who as an old comrade of the Pacificator, gave the party a dinner. The town is on the side of a mountain, and to reach it they passed a fierce torrent over a fragile shaking wooden bridge. Of this river, also, we learn no more, and are uncertain, therefore, whether the dividing land of the waters of India had yet been reached. They were overtaken here by two imperial couriers, who had left Lassa only six days before, and had in that short time accomplished six hundred miles, on the same road that the missionaries had traversed with so much difficulty in a month. Our travellers were told that the dispatches would reach Pekin on the thirtieth day, carried all the way frequently by the same men. The couriers who make these wonderful journeys, prepare themselves by a day of fast before starting, and during the whole journey eat only two eggs at each relay, never resting anywhere, and travelling both night and day.

There are two monasteries at Chobando, and

in one is the great printing press for sacred
works for the entire Kham province, which they
had now entered. Kia-Yu-Kiao was the next
station; the road led down a valley of heavy forest,
and the river Look-chou, which flows through
it was broad, deep and rapid; the wooden bridge
over it had recently fallen, the wood having de-
cayed from age and neglect. The river was accordingly passed on a raft constructed hastily for
the purpose. Nine or ten miles below Kia-yu-
Kiao they crossed the river again over a fragile
wooden bridge, and then passed over a mountain to Wa-ho-chai, a military station, where it
began to snow heavily, much to the discomfiture
and alarm of the caravan, for the next day's march
lay over a frozen lake, where a general with all his
army had been buried in snow in the reign of
Kang-hi, owing to his firing a gun at the time of
encamping according to the regulated order of the
Chinese military service. The march of next day
was long, being one hundred and fifty lis, or from
forty-five to fifty miles. They started before day-
light, and crossed the table-land and lake of Wa-ho
in full sunshine, their eyes suffering extremely
from the glare of the snow, notwithstanding
their use of hair spectacles. It was dark before
they came to an end of the table-land, and they
reached Nzenda-chai, by a painful descent, at mid-

night, completely worn out with fatigue and nearly blinded. They were compelled to halt next day, in order to relieve their eyes by medical treatment· After three more stages of severe mountain travel' they reached Chamdo (Tsiamdo) on the banks of the great river, Kiang-tang-Chou. Thus, in thirty-six days from Lassa, they had got over two thousand five hundred lis, of the Chinese itinerary, which they reckoned equal to two hundred and fifty leagues, or seven hundred and fifty miles. A li is not quite one-third of a mile, for two hundred lis equal a degree of latitude, or sixty-nine miles, one hundred and sixty-six decimals.

Chamdo is a considerable military station: it has a garrison of three hundred men, with four officers, a Yeon-Ki, a Tsien-Choong, and two Pa-Choongs. There is also a depôt of provisions, under charge of a civil officer called a Liang-tai. Chamdo is the capital of the province of Kham, and was heretofore fortified, but the walls had fallen to decay. It lies in the fork of the two rivers, Dza-Chou and Om-Chou, which uniting form the Kiang-tou-chou, which flows into Cambodia, and is there called the Ya-long-Kiang; both are bridged, and the road from Lassa to Se-Chouen passes over one, that to Yunan over the other bridge. Chamdo is a considerable city, but rather in decay. There is a large Lamaserai under a Kotooktoo, who is the sovereign of the Kham province. Inferior to him but also of saintly dignity, is the Chak-Chouba of Jaya, a Lamaserai, lying five hundred lis, or one hundred and fifty miles eastward towards China. At the period of our missionaries passing through Chamdo there was a feud raging between its Kotooktoo and this Chak-chouba; the latter, an aspiring young priest, claimed to have received the diploma of a Kotooktoo in a previous generation, from the Delai Lama, a fact of which it was difficult to prove the negative. The Chamdo Kotooktoo, however, refused to recognise this assumption of new dignities, and the entire province, and especially the priesthood of Kham, were in commotion on account of this quarrel. After the usual course of written and verbal disputation in support of the claim and in resistance to it, the partisans of each side came to blows. Half the province had been ravaged by these hostilities, and the bitterness with which the war was carried on convulsed the entire population. A truce had recently been agreed to, at the time when our missionaries passed, in order that the quarrel might be referred for adjudication to the Delai Lama, and commissioners had been sent from Lassa, and from Pekin, to adjust the difference. Many conferences had, in consequence, been held, and the young aspirant of Jaya himself attended at Chamdo

with a large retinue of his adherents to influence
and overawe the decision. The popular feeling
was all on his side, the elder Kotooktoo of Chamdo
being deemed a creature of the imperial court of
Pekin, and the Tibetan national spirit eschewing
especially, all foreign intervention in their spiritual quarrels. The missionaries were treated with
deference and respect by both parties during the
three days of their halt at Chamdo. The infirmi-
ties of Lee, the Pacificator of Kingdoms, and especially the swelling of his legs, had so increased
during this painful journey, that he was advised
here to purchase a palanquin, but could not be induced to incur the expense. The party was overtaken at this stage by a Chinese Liang-tou, or
civil commissary, who was returning to China with
his son, a youth of eighteen years of age; both
travelled in palanquins, having left Lassa a few
days after the missionaries: but they had suffered
so much from the journey, that it was doubtful
whether they would have strength to reach their
native country.

On our travellers leaving Chamdo, their party was
joined by a Chinese soldier, who, having received
his discharge, was carrying back his family by a
Tibetan wife—an unusual thing, for which he was
laughed at by the men of the Chinese escort. The
wife rode an ass, and led a pack-horse with a child

in each of two cages balanced across his back.
The soldier brought up the rear, with a boy of
twelve years old riding behind him. The route of
the caravan lay up the Dza-Chou river to Meng-
Phoo, distant only about twenty-five miles, and
next day a march of twenty miles brought them
to Pao-tun, where the Tibetan population began
to show a hostile spirit towards the Chinese of the
escort. A march of thirty miles then carried
them to Bagong; in the course of it they saw
many calcareous hills, full of natural caves, some
of large dimensions, but they could not stop to
examine them. Before this, all the mountains the
missionaries had crossed from Lassa were of gra-
nite, but now most of them were of chalk or
lime-stone, and the road near Bagong was skirted
with frequent slabs of marble, on which the mys-
terious prayer " Om mani padme hom " was
carved, with more or less neatness, in evidence of
the devotion of the population.

On the road between Chamdo and Bagong the
Chinese Liang-Tou died in his palanquin; the
bearers on setting it down and opening the cur-
tains found him dead. He had left Chamdo two
days only before the caravan; and the son here
purchased a coffin, and fixed it in the palanquin,
in order that the corpse might be so conveyed to
the land of its fathers. For this the young man

paid dearly, but filial duty required the sacrifice.

The Tibetan authorities at Bagong distinctly
told Lee the Pacificator, that no oola would be
furnished except on payment of a fixed rate of
hire. The Pacificator remonstrated, but it was
of no use. He accordingly made a complaint
to the Proul-Tamba, a Tibetan Lama of great
influence, who lived at a short distance from
Bagong. The Lama came himself the next day,
and was received with great ceremony. He was a
man of much intelligence, and of very striking appearance. He recognised the Pacificator as an old
comrade, but was himself a hot partisan of the
Jaya-Kotooktoo, and had been engaged in many
warlike operations in his favour, in which he had
always been victorious. He complained loudly of
the Chinese for having interfered in the domestic
quarrels of Kham, and alluded also to the trial
and punishment of the Nom-Khan of Lassa by
Ki-Shen, as a gross violation of Tibetan indepen-
dence. He even spoke slightingly of the great
emperor, as being a layman of no equal authority
with a regenerate Boodh. After much invective
of the same kind against Chinese domination, he
gave at last the oola out of consideration for his
old comrade, and for the two Lamas of the West,
who he said had been specially recommended to

him by the regent of Lassa. Their route lying by
the residence of the Proul-Tamba, they paid him a
visit of ceremony on their way, in return for this
civility, and towards evening arrived at Wang-Tsa,
where the Chinese guardhouse had been demolished
and everything showed signs of civil war. Here
the men who came with the oola resigned their
charge to the women of the place, because Gaya,
the next stage, being of the opposite faction, the
men dared not show themselves near it. On their
arrival at Gaya, the women delivered their charge,
and returned immediately with the oola quite un-
molested, leaving the travellers at the mercy of
the population. A council was forthwith held of
the chief men of the place, and it was resolved to
furnish an oola to the Tibetans of the party, and
to the missionaries, gratis, in deference to the
regent of Lassa, but to demand payment for all
animals taken by Chinese of the party. The
Pacificator remonstrated, and inveighed in vain
against this resolution; he was obliged to submit.

At Angti, the next stage, they were detained five
days, partly by a fall of snow, but mainly while
discussing the affair of the oola. The Deba Chief
of Angti, was a dwarf, almost without legs, named
Bomba, a man nevertheless of great energy of
character. Mounted on the shoulders of a strong
mountaineer, his voice was always heard loudest;

he influenced every determination of the local council, and arranged everything. He also was particularly civil to the missionaries, and gave them a dinner, but was inexorable in his hostility to the Chinese.

On leaving Angti there is a high snowy mountain pass, which proved as troublesome as any of the preceding. The passage occupied the whole day, and it was midnight before they reached Jaya, the head quarters of the aspiring Kotooktoo. The town had suffered in the civil war, and was nearly destroyed; but there was here a guardhouse and a garrison of twenty Chinese, who strove almost in vain to maintain a strict neutrality in the civil war. The next stage was Adzoo-Than, where they overtook, again, the palanquin of the Liang-Tou, who had died at Bagong, and whose son here also fell a victim to the hardships of the journey. How to carry to China this second corpse, puzzled much the ingenuity of the escort, yet it was a duty not to be neglected. The body of the son was accordingly secretly cut in pieces, and placed in the same coffin with the father.

From Adzoo-Thang the next stage was Ché-Pan-Keou, a valley of slates, gold-dust, and musk deer. Here, and at the three following stations, the Chinese were similarly called upon to pay the hire of the oola, while the missionaries and Tibetans were furnished with cattle gratis.

The party next arrived at Keang-Tsa, a Chinese town and military post of considerable size, having two military mandarins. These latter persuaded Lee, the Pacificator, to give up travelling on horseback, and to use the palanquin of the son of the civilian, which was at his service gratis, in consequence of the youth's decease.

Four days after leaving Keang-Tsa, the caravan reached the banks of the mighty Yang-tse-Keang. They crossed it soon after, and descended its valley to Bathang, a large city and military station, situated in a climate differing altogether from that in which they had spent the preceding two years. At Bathang is a garrison of three hundred Chinese soldiers, under a Chiou-Pie, two Tsien-Chongs, and a Pa-Choong, whose pay, amounting in the whole to nine thousand ounces of silver, is remitted regularly from China. The population is mixed Chinese and Tibetan. There is here a large Tibetan Lamaserai, under a Kampo-delegate of the Delai Lama, but his authority is confined to spiritual matters, the temporal power being in the hands of a Tou-Tse, or tributary prince of China. The increasing illness of the Pacificator caused a halt of three days at Bathang. From Chamdo to Bathang the route had been southerly for the entire twenty days of march, but now it turned northward, and on the second day after leaving that city, they crossed

another snowy range, and encamped in a miserable
hut, at a station called Ta-so, situated in a valley,
whence again they ascended, next day, to a table-
land covered with snow. Beneath it was a magnificent forest of pines, and cedars, and hollies of
large size.

The march was long from Ta-so to Samba, and
Lee, the Pacificator, quite worn out with the
fatigue, was found dead in his bed in the morning.
This caused a halt, until arrangements could be
made to carry the body forward. The Chinese
escort were now without a commandant, and
were not willing to obey the Tibetan Lama, who
had the separate charge of the escort of that
nation, provided by the regent of Lassa. The
missionaries were compelled in consequence to
take on themselves the general direction of the
party, and were cheerfully obeyed by the men of
both nations. Three more days of mountain
march carried them to Li-thang, a depot with one
hundred soldiers, having for officers a Liang-tai,
a Cheon-pie, and two Pa-Choongs. It was the
duty of one of these to take the command vacated
by the death of the Pacificator, and to carry on
the escort, but all wished to shirk the service, and
to leave the missionaries to direct the march, as
they had done since the death of the brigadier-
general. On their refusal, a Pa-Choong was at

last appointed, who begged for a delay of two days to make preparation.

At Li-thang is a printing-press for Boodhist sacred books, but the language of the place is neither Tibetan nor Chinese, and seemed to the missionaries to resemble the Sifan dialect of the Kokonoor more than any other. The Tibetans of the escort were understood with difficulty. From Li-thang to Ta Tsien-lou, the frontier town of Sechouen, was a further distance of six hundred lis, or two hundred miles, of mountain road, divided into eight stages. In the course of this march, one day beyond Makian-Joong, the party crossed a large tributary of the Yang-tse-Kiang, called Ya-loong-Kiang, which rises at the foot of the Bayan Kharat Mountains, and joins the Blue River in the Sechouen province. At Ta-Tsien-lou the Tibetan escort took leave. It was the end of June when this town was reached; the journey from Lassa having occupied three months, and being rated in Chinese itineraries at five thousand and fifty lis, sixteen hundred and eighty-three miles. From thence to Sechouen the missionaries tra-velled in palanquins. Of their adventures there, and the trial they underwent before the Chinese tribunals, they promise a separate report, which, if the story be but half as well told as this of their journeys in Tartary and Tibet, will be looked for and read with double interest ; for M. Huc's lively and unpretending narrative cannot fail to leave in every reader most kindly feelings of respect for the character of these missionaries, joined to a high reverence for the truly apostolic zeal, and untiring energy which carried them through their hardships.   Every one therefore will desire to follow them through all their further dangers, and to learn every circumstance of their relations with the singular sections of the human race, with which they were brought thus strangely in collision, and of whose institutions, habits and feelings their narrative promises to afford a more perfect knowledge.

But of all the important matters laid. open to us in these volumes, there is nothing so interesting, or so deserving of attention, as the insight they afford into the Boodhist doctrines, and into the discipline, ritual, and practices of those who still believe and profess that religion.   We must not close our notice of this work without reverting to this subject.

Every body knows that the Boodhist faith so widely spread over Eastern Asia, had its origin in the teachings of Sakhya Muni, a saint, whose era dates long before Christ.   The Chinese carry the era back to more than one thousand years. De Guignes and Klaproth fix it from these autho-

rities at 1027 years before Christ; and Sir William
Jones adopted the same date. But it is to be
observed, that the Chinese, acknowledging the
author of this religion to have been a native of
India, state their nation to have adopted the faith
of Boodh one thousand years after it had been
preached there. Their chronology, therefore, so
far as it dates from this era, commenced only from
the thousandth year, and wants earlier verification.
Indian authorities, on the other hand, confirming
the Cingalese, Burmese, and Siamese dates for the
commencement of the Boodhist era, fix the death
of Sakhya-Muni (called his *nirvan,* or absorption
into the divine spirit) in the year B.C. 543.
This difference of four hundred and thirty-six
years has led many to believe the Chinese era to
refer to an anterior Boodh, but it is more probably
ascribable to the round number of a thousand, assumed for the antiquity of the religion at the time
of its spread in that country. The date is so far
important, as the extraordinary similitude in many
parts of the doctrine, and of the books, and ritual,
and forms, and institutions of this religion, with
those of Romish Christianity, which was remarked
by the Jesuits who visited Tibet in the seventeenth
century, and even by Father Rubruquis in the
thirteenth, might lead to the belief that they had
been borrowed entirely from this latter, if the

chain of evidence that established their greater antiquity were less complete.

The points of resemblance referred to commence even with the form of the Scriptures, or principal books of the faith. The most important is the life of Sakhya-Muni, whose doctrines are represented as having been delivered in discourses held to his ten disciples, or as arising out of occasions not unsimilar in some respects to those recorded in our Evangelists. The idea of a divine spirit being moved to take on itself a human form for the instruction of mankind, and for the redemption of the human race from the sins into which it had fallen by a course of degeneracy, is Boodhistical. The doctrine of the fall of man, that is, the Mosaic account of the creation of the world, and of the original sin of the father of the human race, is no part of Boodhism; and this we may remark would likewise most probably have been found there, if it had been a religion borrowed from the Christian as its antecedent. The spirit of Sakhya-Muni is alleged to have been pre-existent, in a condition of sanctified holiness, pre-eminent amongst the gods of Tushita, and there, being moved to become incarnate in the human form, in order to redeem mankind from the sin and degeneracy it had fallen into from long tasting of earthly pleasures, and from their corrupting influences, it elected the royal

race of Shudhoduna for the birth. The conception of Maya-Devi, the mother, is described as miraculous and mystical, and the birth as attended
with miracles, but not of the same description with
those which attended the birth of our Saviour.
There is, however, a holy man like Simeon, who,
admonished by an illumination of the world, bears
witness to the child's divine mission, and laments
that age will prevent his hearing his doctrine.
Sakhya also at school displays learning which con-
founds the doctors and professors. He takes on
himself the domestic state, and marries twice, but
at the age of twenty-nine, he is led to commence
a course of meditation, his attention being directed
to four subjects in particular—old age, sickness,
death, and a future state. He gives up the world
to pursue his meditations on these subjects, and
to seek the truth. He practises mortifications,
until finding his body weakened, he bathes in the
Nyranjana river, and takes refreshment afterwards
to recover his strength. This is a species of baptism. He is tempted after his baptism by the
God of Pleasure, who makes offers of worldly
power, like those we find in the Temptation in the
Wilderness. But he rejects them, and overcomes
and drives away the tempter. After this his meditations are rewarded by an inspiration of the
divine Spirit, and so becoming a supreme Boodh,

he begins to preach his doctrine, which is adopted first by ten disciples of implicit faith, and then wins over the multitude.

The precepts he inculcates are:—First, That there is sorrow in life. Second, That this sorrow is inseparable from mortality. Third, That it may be remedied. Fourth, That faith in his doctrine, and its reception and observance will give the remedy, which is, salvation in an improved future state, preparatory to absorption ultimately in the divine spirit. He goes from place to place in India, teaching this doctrine, and is followed and revered, until he dies at last in Assam at the advanced age of eighty, his death being attended with many prodigies. The body is burnt, and the remains collected and revered as relics of pre-eminent sanctity. A contention then arises, as to their disposal, and the remains are divided between eight cities, each of which erects a Stupa, or mausoleum over its portion.

This is said to have occurred in the reign of Ajata-Satra, who was the predecessor of Chandragupta (Sandracottus) by one hundred and ninety-six years. The future state promised by Sakhya-Muni, is regeneration in an inferior or superior animal condition, according to the degree of spiritual perfection obtained in life by meditation and faith, the highest reward of all being that which

Sakhya-Muni himself obtained, viz., absorption
into the divine Spirit, from which all vitality is
believed to have emanated originally, and to which
all will finally return. The next highest state to
that of immediate absorption, is that of perpetual
regeneration as a Boodh. There is in Boodhism
no perpetuity of punishment in a place of torments,
but the regeneration in inferior animals, is not
very dissimilar to the purgatory of Catholics, as
was remarked by Father Grueber; and the Devas,
or gods, of the different heavens, are of the same
class with angels and saints. In every state there
is a means of reaching a superior condition, if
properly followed out; and life is sacred and not
to be taken without sin, because of its being of the
divine essence, passing, in this world, through the
course prescribed towards final absorption.

Such are the principal characteristics of the
Boodhist doctrine. With respect to the institutions: the doctrine that a spiritual and even a
divine condition is to be obtained by withdrawing
from the world, and by meditation, prayer, and
abstraction, gave early origin to the monastic condition. We have distinct evidence of the existence
of institutions of this kind established in viharas,
or cells and caves, or in buildings, erected for the
convenience of those who sought so to spiritualise
themselves by separation from the world, at dates

long antecedent to our era. Such buildings exist
in India, at present, only as remains of antiquity,
quite deserted; but we find them in Tibet and
Tartary, exactly in the condition that we may
imagine, from the traces left of the domiciles occupied by the Indian Sramanas, or Lamas, that they
presented heretofore in various parts of Hindoo-
stan: and this at periods, at least twenty centuries anterior to the present. That condition
varies very little from what is reported of the
earlier Christians; and we have still, according to
M. Huc, both at Koon-boom and in Tibet, the
type of the devotees who practised penances, and
sat on pillars, like Simeon Stelites.

The discipline, the habits, and even the ritual of
these monasteries of Tibet and Tartary have also
a remarkable resemblance to those of the churches
of Rome and Constantinople in the middle ages.
With respect to the ritual, we have before noticed
the strong impression which its resemblance in
many points made on Father Grueber, in the seventeenth century. Captain Turner, the ambassador of Warren Hastings to Tibet, in 1783, remarked the great similarity which the chaunts of
alternate verses by the officiating priest, and by
the congregations of Tibet, bore to the ceremonies
of high-mass in the Roman Church. He was
quite ignorant of the Tibetan language, and

judged merely of the form, and manner, and effect
of what he saw and heard. M. Huc confirms this
report, as the result of his longer and more accurate observation, based on some acquaintance
with the language of Tibet; and he tells us how
intense and extensive is the study of ritual in the
Koon-boom monastic college, and in similar institutions of Lassa. Now Csoma de Koros has given
us translations, and abstracts, of some part of
what is thus chaunted or recited, and we have
ourselves been much struck by the resemblance in
spirit and tone, to parts of the Litany, and of the
Psalms, which are similarly read or chaunted in
Catholic churches. Take the following hymn, for
instance, in celebration of the victory gained over
the great tempter, prior to the reception of the
divine inspiration by Sakhya-Muni. We copy
it from Csoma de Koros' translation, breaking
only the verses, for alternation of the chaunt or
recitation, which is the method of reading and
delivering it.

Priest. " There has arisen the Illuminator of the
world ! the world's Protector ! the Maker of light;
who gives eyes to the world that is blind,—to cast
away the burden of sin."

Congregation. " Thou hast been victorious in the
fight : thy aim is accomplished by thy moral

excellence : thy virtues are perfect : Thou shalt
satisfy men with good things."

P. " Gotama (Sakhya) is without sin : He is
out of the miry pit. He stands on dry ground."

C. " Yes, He is out of the mire ; and he will save
other animated beings, that are carried off by the
mighty stream."

P. " The living world has long suffered the disease of corruption. The Prince of physicians is
come to cure men from all diseases."

C. " Protector of the world ! by thy appearance,
all the mansions of distress shall be made empty.
Henceforth, angels and men shall enjoy happi-
ness," &c. &c.

Again, see another hymn.

Priest. " To Thee, whose virtue is immaculate,
whose understanding is pure and brilliant, who
hast the thirty-two characteristic signs complete,
and who hast memory of all things, with discern-
ment and fore-knowledge."

Congregation. " Reverence be to Thee : we adore
Thee ; bending our heads to our feet."

P. " To Thee, who art clean and pure from all
taint of sin,—who art immaculate, and celebrated
in the three worlds,—who, being possessed of the
three kinds of science, givest to animated beings

the eye to discern the three degrees of emancipation from sin."

C. "Reverence be to Thee."

P. "To Thee, who with tranquil mind clearest the troubles of evil times : who, with loving kindness, teachest all living things to walk in the path designed for them."

C. "Reverence be to Thee!"

P. "Muni! whose heart is at rest, and who delightest to explain the doubts and perplexities of men : who hast suffered much for the good of living beings : Thy intention is pure! Thy practices are perfect."

C. "Reverence be to Thee."

P. "Teacher of the four truths; rejoice in salvation! who, being thyself free from sin, desirest to free the world from sin."

C. "Reverence be to Thee."

We could multiply illustrations of this kind without limit, but these examples will suffice to show the resemblance we have noticed in the forms and method of the Boodhist ritual. It is, however, much more elaborate than that of any church of Christendom, the books containing it being very voluminous, and the services being exceedingly complicated, and differing, almost, for every day of the year, besides being special for every festival.

In the absence of authentic histories, it is not easy to settle the precise period when the doctrine and forms of Boodhist worship were first established in the east; but no one has ever doubted their great antiquity. The early missionaries of the Romish church believed them to be a form of Christianity preached there in the time of the first Apostles; and hearing of the theocratic government established in Tibet, and occasionally amongst Tartars and Mongols of the desert, carried back to Europe tales of a Prester, or Presbyter John, to excite the wonder and stimulate the zeal of the pious in Christendom. But the more accurate and searching enquiries of the present age have brought out this religion in a new character, and leave little doubt of its priority by several centuries to Christianity, with forms of worship and with doctrines, corresponding closely with those which so forcibly struck Captain Turner in Tibet, and which excited the wonder of the missionaries of successive centuries, both there and in Mongolia.

Of the sacred books of Boodhism we have now three complete versions, in the Sanscrit, Tibetan, and Pali languages; and all have been carefully examined and reported upon by thorough proficients in each of these languages respectively. We have a Sanscrit version that was obtained in Nipal by Mr. Hodgson, the British resident at Katman-

H

doo,and after being studied and partially abstracted
by himself, was by him transmitted to the Royal
Library of Paris about fifteen years ago, and has
there been closely examined by Messrs. Remusat
and Bournouf, whose works on the subject are
before the world. We have also a Tibetan version
obtained through the same channel, and subjected
by the government of India to the examination of
M. Csoma da Koros. The result of his labours has
appeared in several translations and abstracts,which
were published in the Asiatic Researches of Bengal,
and in the monthly journal of the Asiatic Society
between the years 1835 and 1840. The Pali version
was traced out by Mr. Wm. Turnour, a high civil
functionary of Ceylon.   This gentleman first published in a separate volume the text, with a close
translation of the Maha-wansa, an ancient poem on
the origin and spread of the Boodhist religion, compiled in the fifth century of our era from the Cingalese version of the Attha-katha, a work of much
higher antiquity. He next published in the pages
of the journal of the Asiatic Society of Bengal, a
series of valuable essays, with the heading of " Pali
Budhistical Annals;" and in these we find a complete analysis of the sacred books themselves, and
a critical examination of the grounds for assuming
them to be genuine, and for assigning them to a
date and period very nearly corresponding with

that claimed for them by the professors of the religion.

We have no means of determining the precise date when the Sanscrit version of these Boodhist Scriptures was prepared. It professes to have been made from an original in the language of Moghada, that is, of Bahar, in which province both Pataliputra, (the ancient Palibothra, now Patna) and Rajgriha, where Sakhya Muni was born, and which was the more ancient capital of that province, were situated. The Tibetan version was translated from the Sanscrit, and took the shape of the Kahgyur, in which it now exists, in one hundred leaf volumes, between the seventh and ninth centuries of our era. Tibet does not pretend to conversion to Boodhism till many centuries after the death of Sakhya Muni; we cannot, therefore, look in this quarter for evidence of the date of the first appearance of this religion in the world; but when we find that the version of its Scripture now current there, and the Sanscrit version also, through which it was derived, correspond in all essentials with the Pali version of the same Scripture found in Ceylon, Siam, and Burma (for all these are identical), it is an undeniable collateral evidence of the genuine character of the whole; for there could be no collusion between the priests of all these distant regions. Still, in order to establish the antiquity of the original

Scriptures, we must seek other proofs than this conformity.

The Pali books examined and abstracted by Mr. Turnour, consist of the Pitakattayan, the Attha-katha, and the Mahawansa. The first is, *quasi*, the gospel of Boodhists, containing the life, discourses and precepts of Sakhya Muni himself, as derived from his own mouth, and put together by his disciples immediately after his decease. The Attha-katha is, *quasi*, the acts of the Apostles, and contains the account of the settlement of the Pitakattayan, and of the succession of Theros, or chief disciples and preachers of the religion after Sakhya Muni; also of the schisms which took place in the first few centuries after the *nirvan*, or decease, of the great saint and founder; and especially of the convocations held, as well to settle the Gospel itself in the first instance, as to determine the points of difference, and to suppress the schisms as they arose. This latter work is by far the most valuable to the historian, and if its genuineness and antiquity can be considered established, there are many doubtful points of chronology, and many matters touching the succession of kingly races, and of events, also regarding the state of society of the period between the death of Sakhya, B.C. 543, and the date of its promulgation, B. c. 306, that it will assist in clearing up.

It is stated in the Mahawansa, that the Pitakattayan was brought to Ceylon by Mahindo, the son
of Asoka, in the eighteenth year of his father's
reign, that is, in B. C. 306, in the exact Pali form
in which it now exists. That the Attha-katha was
brought to the island at the same time, but was
circulated and first made known in the Cingalese
vernacular dialect. Both books are stated to have
been preserved orally only for more than two centuries, as they well might be in the monasteries;
but to have been committed to writing in the reign
of a king who flourished in Ceylon between B. C.
104 and B. C. 76. The Attha-katha existed in this
condition in Cingalese, until it was rendered back
into Pali by a priest who came from Moghada, of
great learning and celebrity, whose name was Budha
Ghosa. This is stated to have occurred between
the years A. D. 410, and A. D. 432; and a full account of all these circumstances is given in the Mahawansa, which was written between A.D. 459, and
A.D. 477, and which professes to have been compiled
from the same Cingalese version of the Attha-katha.
The facts mentioned in both these works correspond
in all essentials with the record of similar events
found in the Sanscrit and Tibetan sacred books,
and the differences consist only of some insertions
in the former, specially referring to Ceylon, and
likely to have been interpolated by priests of that

nation. We may, therefore, fairly look on these
works as standing nearly on the same footing as
the Pitakattayan : for the record of events found
in them was equally brought to Ceylon in the reign
of Asoka, in the condition in which it existed, and
was received and believed in Moghada in that
reign. This, be it observed, was more than three
hundred years before the birth of our Saviour.
The Attha-katha contains nothing of subsequent
date to B. c. 306, and it appears to have come
to us perfect through this channel, although not
free from interpolations, and not in the original
text.

Now, let us examine whether these books contain internal evidence to confirm the inference that
they were current at this early period. The Pitakattayan, which contains the life and discourses
of Sakhya Muni, refers to cotemporary kings of
India, of dynasties known then to have held dominion in India, and to disciples of Sakhya, who became afterwards leaders of the Boodhist faith.
There is nothing found in it inconsistent with the
fact of its declared antiquity. The Attha-katha
tells us that this Pitakattayan was settled in the
state in which we find it, for the Pali language corresponds with that of Moghada, at a convocation
held in the first year after Sakhya's decease ; three
of his disciples, Kasyapa, Upali, and Anando,

having each presided at the recital and settlement of the three several portions of the work.

This account of its authorship is confirmed precisely by what is found in the Sanscrit and Tibetan versions of the same sacred books. The Pali Attha-katha tells us further of schisms which then arose amongst the professors of the Boodhist religion, and that for the settlement of these, a second convocation was held one hundred years after the first, which determined the points in dispute, and expelled the heretics. Of this convocation, however, and of the schisms which led to it, we have no mention in the Tibetan scriptures of Boodhism, which, as they were avowedly of much later origin, would seem to show that the importance of the convocation, and perhaps even the memory of the schism, had then quite passed away. The points in dispute in this first century of Boodhism, referred to indulgences in matters of priestly discipline, such as in respect to the keeping of salt for more than seven days, which some pretended might be allowed in vessels of horn; also in the eating of food after mid-day, and things of the kind. The indulgences claimed were ten in number. The convocation denounced them all, requiring a rigid adherence to the letter as well as to the spirit of the rules and precepts of the Pitakattayan,

as settled at the first convocation, which shows
the severe discipline enforced at that early period
in all viharas, as the religious establishments of
the priesthood were then called in India.

In the reign of Asoka, the grandson of Chandragupta, who was the Sandracottus of Megasthenes, a third convocation was held, according
to the Attha-katha and Mahawansa, and the Tibetan sacred books confirm this. King Asoka is
stated to have become a convert to Boodhism in
the fourth year of his reign, and was an active
propagandist of the faith. The Attha-katha says,
that consequently upon this royal patronage, many
heretics and unbelievers assumed the priestly garb,
" shaving their heads and clothing themselves in
yellow robes," which is exactly the characteristic
of Lamas of the present day; and that they
sauntered about viharas, spreading dissensions
and interrupting the ceremonies of the true religion, being especially addicted to fire-worship
and to sacrifices. Consequently, upon these dissensions, the rigid priests of Boodhism suspended
the performance of the " Uposâtho " periodical
worship and ceremonies, and also of the Pawa-
râno, declaring that these could not properly be
performed in the public halls or churches of the
viharas in company with heretics. The suspension of these rites continued, according to the

statement, for seven years, when King Asoka, taking umbrage, ordered the Uposâtho to be renewed at his principal vihara at Pataliputra, and sent his chief minister to enforce this order. The heads of the establishment still refused, whereupon the minister caused several of them to be beheaded on the spot, in the order in which they sat in the assembly. The king's brother, Tisso, who was attached to this vihara, then placed himself on the seat to which the minister next came in turn, and held out his head for martyrdom by decapitation; but the minister hesitated, and referred again to the king for orders. Shocked at the issue to which the matter had thus been brought, King Asoka humbled himself before the ministers of religion, and asked for absolution. A convocation was then held to settle the points in dispute, and the Boodhist church being purged by the expulsion of 60,000 heretics, whose yellow dresses were taken away and white furnished to them instead, the Uposâtho was performed again with great solemnity. It was at this convocation that the sacred books were again revised and finally settled, and the Attha-katha closes with the record of this particular event. It occurred in the seventeenth year after Asoka's inauguration, that is, in the year B.C. 307, just before Mahindo's mission to Ceylon.

Such, but with extraordinary detail, is the internal evidence deducible from these sacred books
of Ceylon. It remains to show how this evidence
is supported by external events and circumstances.
There is, first, the fact of the era of the death of
Sakhya Muni (called his "Nirvan" or absorption into the divinity), which era, being introduced into Ceylon at the time of Mahindo's carrying thither the religion and scriptures of Boodhism,
has been retained in the annals of that island to
the present day. The same era is current in
Burma and in Siam. There is, second, the re-
ference to the reign of Chandragupta and his
descendants, whose identity with the Sandracottus of Megasthenes is admitted, and whose
reign is thus fixed chronologically. These are
strong corroborative circumstances, but are far
from being the whole of the evidence. Within
the last fifteen years, inscriptions in a very ancient
Indian character have been deciphered, which
purport to be edicts of a king who calls himself
Devanam-pia-Piadasi. These edicts, as translated by Mr. James Prinsep, with the aid of pundits in Calcutta, purport to be injunctions of a
direct Boodhist character, consistent with the
faith thus stated to have been adopted by King
Asoka ; and Mr. Turnour has identified the
name of Piadasi as identical with that of King

Asoka. In two copies of these edicts, viz., those
found at Girnar in Guzrat, and at Kapoordigiri,
not far from Peshawur, the names of Antiochus
and Ptolemy, and of Antigonus, Alexander, and
Magas, are specifically cited as of cotemporary
kings, through whom the doctrines and principles
of the edicts are to be further extended. We are
aware that Professor Wilson, in a recent memoir
on these inscriptions, has cast doubts on the interpretation of the edicts, and denies that there is
ground for assigning them to King Asoka, or
even for supposing them to be Boodhistical; but
his criticism is a mere statement of doubts; and
whether the edicts of the specific inscription he
discusses, which is five times repeated, and pur-
ports to contain the edicts of the twenty-seventh
year of Piadasi's reign, be fairly susceptible of
Boodhistical interpretation or no, signifies little,
for there is a further edict in the same precise
language and character, and of the same King
Pyadasi, which was discovered at Bhabra, on
the road between Jypore and Dehli, and which
settles the point by specifically referring to the
precepts and doctrines of "Bhagavat Boodha,"
the Lord Boodha, as the only faith to be followed,
and condemns the precepts of the Vedas, which
enjoin sacrifices; and the same edict especially
upholds the merit and virtues of the "Uposadh"

ceremonies, and further, is specifically addressed to the faithful congregated in Moghada. It would thus seem to have been published in the seventeenth year of this king, on the conclusion of the convocation, referred to in the Attha-katha, for purging the Boodhist church of Vedan heresies, as the condition upon which only the Boodhist priesthood would perform the periodically-recurring rite of Uposadh. This* inscription will be found in No. 102 of the Journal of the Asiatic Society of Calcutta, and is there given in text, with a translation by Kamla Kant and Sarodha Prashad, the same pundits who assisted Mr. James Prinsep in the translation and deciphering of the edicts before discovered. The stone containing the

---

* The following extracts are from the translation of this most important edict, as made by Kamla Kanta Pundit and Sarodha Prashad :—

" Piadasa Raja, to the multitude assembled in Maghada, saluting them, says thus:—

" That the sacrifice of animals is forbidden is well known to you. For men of Boodhist faith, such is not mete. The performance of the Uposadh is most essential."

" The vedas of the Munis are observed by their disciples ; their future state is to be dreaded.
" The text of the vedas enjoining sacrifices are mean and false. Follow what the Lord Boodha hath commanded. Do this for the glory of Dhurma (religion). This I desire," &c.

writing was afterwards transmitted to Calcutta,
and is there deposited. The Uposadh was a re-
curring monthly rite, regulated by the moon's
changes; it was a church service performed in
the public halls of the viharas, and whether it
could properly be performed in private houses was
one of the schismatic points settled at the second
convocation. Its suspension for seven years was
felt as a national grievance, which the King Asoka
determined to remedy, but he was compelled by
the obstinacy of the priesthood to submit to their
condition of first cleansing the church of its heretics and schismatics. We conceive, that upon
this collateral testimony of rock-preserved edicts,
in a language no longer extant, but conforming
with that of the Pali sacred books of Ceylon,
Siam, and Burma, — of edicts which refer to
kings Ptolemy and Antiochus as cotemporaries,
the inference will not be rejected, that the sacred
books and ritual of the Boodhists, as now observed
by professors of that religion, were then the received scriptures and state religion of India. We
have further evidence of this in the ruins of ancient Stupas and viharas existing in many localities of India, which indicate a condition of things
and of monastic institutions, exactly corresponding with the Lamaserais described as still existing
in Tibet and at Koon-boom, at Koko Khotun, and

in other places of Tartary and Mongolia. The
Stupas are mounds of solid masonry erected over
the ashes or relics of saints and teachers of the
Boodhist religion; and round them cells and
domiciles for disciples or Sramanas appear to have
been built by the pious, or provided by themselves, in the precise manner in which they are
now found at Koonboom and Lassa. These have
for centuries been in ruins, but they bear inscriptions of the same, and even of more early date than
the deciphered edicts of Asoka to which we have
referred above. The most remarkable of these
ruins are found at Sanchi, near Bhilsa, south-
west of Bundelkund. The inscriptions found on
several stones and gateways of this ancient vihara, furnished the key for deciphering the
Asoka edicts; and within these few days, there
has been read at the Royal Asiatic Society of
London, a paper by Captain Cunningham, on the
subject of excavations made to ascertain the precise contents of several of these Stupas. The
metal, steatite, and chrystal vases containing the
relics have all been exhumed, and on several, or
on the covering cerements, are legible inscriptions
in characters of the age antecedent to that of
Asoka, recording that the relics are those of the
very disciples and associates of Sakhya Muni,
whose names are mentioned in the Pitakattayan

and in the Attha-katha, as well as in the Tibetan
books. This seems to be a strong confirmation of
the verity of those books, and of the fact that the
record they contain was at least the received gospel
of the age, when these Stupas were built, and that
alphabet was used. We have no desire and no
right to anticipate the publication of the very interesting results which have attended the search
of these Stupas. Suffice it that they are quite
irreconcileable with any construction of the accounts received of the Boodhist faith, that does
not carry back the founder to the sixth century
before our era. These, indeed, may not be the
real tombs of the saints and disciples of Sakhya
Muni, whose names are found on the vases and
cerements, but the more probable inference is
that they are so; still, whether admitted to be so
or no, the appearance of the buildings, and the
character of the inscriptions, indicates a date for
their construction at least three or four hundred
years before Christ; and the erection of these
Stupas at that date over even fictitious relics,
shows the sacred books recording the laws of
these saints and disciples to be then the received
faith of a large and wealthy population; and this
is all we seek to establish.

If Boodhism, however, existed with these books
at so early a date, we are met by the difficulty of

accounting for the silence of Greek authors of
antiquity in respect to them. The very name of
Boodh is met with nowhere in Greek literature
before the time of Clemens Alexandrinus, and he
mentions only incidentally one Terebinthus, who,
coming from India, set up for a Boodh (βούττα),
and imposed on many. We certainly have difficulty in accounting for this silence, but it is not
inconsistent with Greek habit, so to treat barba-
rian literature of all kinds. How little do we
find in Greek books of the history or literature
of the Persians and Parthians, with whom they
were in close relation, politically and commerci-
ally, for many ages. And it is to be observed, the
Boodhist sacred books were the special property
of the priesthood, and were mostly preserved and
transmitted orally amongst them : probation, by
long discipline, and by shaving the head and
assuming the yellow garb of a priest, was a condition antecedent to the acquisition of any knowledge of them; and the same is even now the case
with rigid Boodhists.   Have not even the learned
of Europe, with the advantage of a press, and a
reading public eager for knowledge, been for
many centuries acquainted with the existence of
Boodhists with peculiar doctrines, without, until
very recently, obtaining any accurate knowledge
of these sacred books?   That the doctrines of

Sakhya Muni spread widely over the western world, as well as over the east, is sufficiently known and established. Pythagoras brought the doctrine of transmigration into Greece at a period so close to that of the decease of Sakhya Muni, as to make it probable that he received it even from himself; but we have no direct evidence that the philosopher went further east than Babylon. The fact, however, that he derived his doctrines from an Indian source is very generally admitted; and it has other points of resemblance with Boodhism, besides the belief in metempsychosis, or transmigration of souls. The discipline he established, and the life of silence and meditation he enjoined, with the degrees of initiation introduced, which was a kind of successive ordination, correspond exactly with the precepts of the Pitakattayan, and the practices reported in the Attha-katha.

The Pythagorean institutions also are described as very monastic in their character, resembling thus closely, in that respect also, the viharas of the Boodhists of India. The doctrines of Pythagoras were widely spread over Greece, over Italy, and Asia Minor for centuries after his decease, and under the name of Mythraic, the faith of Boodh had also a wide extension. The general expectation of the birth of a great prophet, Redeemer, or

162 TIBET, TARTARY

Saviour, which is alluded to even by Tacitus, as
prevailing at the period when the founder of the
Christian religion appeared, was, there can be no
doubt, of Boodhistic origin,* and not at all confined
to Jews, or based only on the prophecies of their
Scripture. Although, therefore, the classic literature of that age affords no evidence of the precise
character of this Boodhism, nor of the basis of
Scripture or tradition on which it rested, still the
two facts, viz., first, the existence of these books in
India at the period ; and secondly, the wide spread
in the west of the doctrines and belief which rested
upon them, may be considered as both well established, and as not likely to be denied.

Under the supposition of the pre-existence of
Boodhism, such as these sacred books describe, and
its professors still preach, the rapid spread of Christianity in the first and second centuries of our era,
is not surprising. To a mind already impressed
with Boodhistic belief and Boodhistic doctrines,
the birth of a Saviour and Redeemer for the Western world, recognised as a new Boodh by wise men

---

* The advent of another Boodh a thousand years after
Gotama, or Sakhya Muni, is distinctly prophesied in the
Pitakattayan and Attha-katha. Gotama declares himself to
be the twenty-fifth Boodh, and says, "Bagawa Metteyo is
yet to come." The name Metteyo bears an extraordinary
resemblance to Messiah.

of the east, that is, by Magi, Sramanas, or Lamas, who had obtained the Arhat sanctification, was an event expected, and therefore readily accepted when declared and announced. It was no abjuration of an old faith that the teachers of Christianity asked of the Boodhists, but a mere qualification of an existing belief by the incorporation into it of the Mosaic account of the creation, and of original sin, and the fall of man. The Boodhists of the west, accepting Christianity on its first announcement, at once introduced the rites and observances which for centuries had already existed in India. From that country Christianity derived its monastic institutions, its forms of ritual, and of church service, its councils or convocations to settle schisms on points of faith, its worship of relics, and working of miracles through them, and much of the discipline, and of the dress of the clergy, even to the shaven heads of the monks and friars. It would require an entire volume to compare in detail the several points of similarity, and to trace the divergence, from the more ancient doctrine and practice, in the creed and forms of ritual ultimately adopted by the churches of the west. It is enough for our present purpose to establish the superior antiquity of the one, found to exhibit so many points of close correspondence.

But independently of the similarity of doctrine

of ritual, and of institutions, we find that Boodhism has run in the east a very analogous course
with Romanism in the west. Having its classes
of specially initiated and ordained teachers, it
spread widely amongst the population, before it
was adopted and made a state religion by the
reigning sovereigns.   It was torn to pieces by
heresies and schisms on trivial observances and
doctrinal points, till one sect, having enlisted the
power of the state on its side, persecuted and expelled its opponents, to the weakening and ulti-
mate ruin of the church and its authority.   The
subserviency of the temporal to the spiritual power
was universally preached by this separate initiated
class; and, in presumptuous reliance on their influence over the populace, priests in the east, as in
the west, have humbled and destroyed the kingly
power, and occasionally, when circumstances favoured the pretension, have established a priestly
government, such as we see in Tibet, in entire
supercession of the ordinary temporal authority,
and have sought to reserve the administration of
all affairs for the special class of initiated or ordained. But the consequence in the east has been
the same as in the west.   The priestly governments have been unable to maintain themselves
without foreign support : priestly domination has
been found quite incompatible with energetic mili-

tary action, which always has been, and always must be, the source of real political power. The great Lamas of Tibet are the protected minions of China, just as the Pope of Rome is dependent to day on France, and was recently on Austria, notwithstanding the reverence in which the Papal name and spiritual authority is still held by vast populations.

But the religion of Tibet and of China, differing widely in that respect from that of papistical Rome, is by principle tolerant. Believing that the human mind can, by meditation and abstraction, arrive at the knowledge of divine truth, it concedes freedom of thought and conscience to all. Boodhists will contend with Boodhists for the superiority of their Kotooktoo, and will persecute and excommunicate those who deny his pretensions. Of this M. Huc witnessed a striking instance in the contentions of the Kotooktoos of Chamdo and of Jaya, as he passed through Kham, the easternmost province of Tibet. But, towards strangers, and the preachers of new doctrines, Boodhists have always displayed not only tolerance, but every desire to hear, to learn, and to understand. Hence the great success that preachers of Christianity have always experienced in their missions to Boodhist countries and communities. Conformity of doctrine and of precepts in several main essentials leads a Boodhist to regard a missionary only as a reformer, nay, even as aiming to reclaim men to the pure or more ancient worship of the best days of his own religion. It is only by alarming the civil authorities, and bringing the government to fear the separate association of large numbers for purposes, and under disciplined leaders, which may be turned to political mischief, that the powers of the state, and of its officers and institutions, are brought into action to suppress and put an end to conversions. They, whose hearts are set on the millenium of a general adoption of the Christian faith, would do well to study the causes which led to the violent persecutions instituted against Christian converts and missionaries, in China, in Japan, and more recently in Cambodia. Let them use their advantage to engraft the belief of the divine mission of Christ on the prepared mind of the Boodhist population, without seeking the separate organization of their converts into communities under a priest's ambitious leading. Let them confine themselves to points of faith, of doctrine, and of morals, without aiming to enforce ritual observances and new modes of life. Thus may they hope to plant the seed, that, sooner or later, will produce a rich harvest of true religious belief, and of virtuous conduct, and sound morality, even though they fail to enforce the universal conformity, which, under the existing diversity of mind, and of motive, and of intellectual power, can scarcely be looked upon as a condition intended by Providence for mankind.

The Boodhist practical creed is thus briefly stated by Csoma da Koros :—

1st. To take refuge only with Boodh.

2nd. To form in the mind the resolution to aim at the highest degree of perfection, and so to be united with the Supreme Intelligence.

3rd. To humble oneself before Boodh, and to adore him.

4th. To make offering of things pleasing to the six senses.

5th. To glorify Boodh by music, and by hymns, and by praise of his person, doctrine, and love of mankind, of his perfections or attributes, and of his acts for the benefit of animated beings.

6th. To confess one's sins with a contrite heart, to ask forgiveness of them, and to repent truly, with a resolution not to commit such afterwards.

7th. To rejoice in the moral merit and perfections of animated beings, and to wish that they may obtain beatitude.

8th. To pray and exhort existing holy men to turn the wheel of religion, that the world may long benefit by their teaching.

Persuade the Boodhist that Christ fulfils his idea of a perfect Boodh, and let the name of Our Saviour be substituted for Boodh, in the above creed, and who will deny that the Boodhist is a perfect Christian.

Tsong-Kaba (Tson-Kha-pa) the saint-reformer of the fourteenth and fifteenth century of our era, according to the same authority, thus defines the duty of Boodhists, classing mankind in three degrees according to their intellectual capacity.

Men of the lowest order of mind must believe that there is a God, and that there is a future life, in which they will receive the reward or punishment of their actions and conduct in this life.

Men of the middle degree of intellectual capacity must add to the above, the knowledge that all things in this world are perishable; that imperfection is a pain and degradation, and that deliverance from existence is a deliverance from pain, and consequently, a final beatitude.

Men of the third, or highest order, must believe in further addition: that nothing exists, or will continue always, or cease absolutely, except through dependence on a causal connection or concatenation. So will they arrive at the true knowledge of God.

What is this but Christianity, wanting only the name of Christ as its preacher, and the Mosaic faith for its antecedent? It is these that the missionary must seek to add.

W. Lewis and Son, Printers, 21, Finch Lane, London.

For EU product safety concerns, contact us at Calle de José Abascal, 56–1°,
28003 Madrid, Spain or eugpsr@cambridge.org.

www.ingramcontent.com/pod-product-compliance
Ingram Content Group UK Ltd.
Pitfield, Milton Keynes, MK11 3LW, UK
UKHW012342130625
459647UK00009B/479